THE
CHURCH
MONEY
MANUAL

Other Abingdon Press Titles by J. Clif Christopher

*Not Your Parents' Offering Plate: A New Vision for
Financial Stewardship*
Whose Offering Plate Is It? New Strategies for Financial Stewardship
Rich Church, Poor Church: Keys to Effective Financial Ministry

THE CHURCH MONEY MANUAL

Best Practices for Finance and Stewardship

J. CLIF CHRISTOPHER

Abingdon Press
Nashville

This book is printed on acid-free paper.

Library of Congress Cataloging-in-Publication Data

Christopher, J. Clif.
    The church money manual : best practices for finances and stewardship / J. Clif Christopher.
        pages   cm
    ISBN 978-1-4267-9657-9 (pbk., trade, binding; soft back : alk. paper)   1. Church finance.   I. Title.
    BV770.C525 2014
    254'8.—dc23

                                                                            2014006338

Disclaimer: All personal names in this book have been changed.

14 15 16 17 18 19 20 21 22 23—10 9 8 7 6 5 4 3 2 1

MANUFACTURED IN THE UNITED STATES OF AMERICA

To the Reverend Doctor Ed Robertson, LTC, USAF (retired), my father-in-law and one of the most amazing men I ever met. He flew over forty different aircraft during World War II, surviving two crashes and countless near misses. He was the only surviving member of his pilot training class. He retired to attend seminary, founding a church that grew to one of the strongest in his state because he went door-to-door sharing the gospel and inviting people to come. He officiated his last baptism at age ninety-one from his hospice bed. He raised four amazing children who carry on his incredible legacy today. He has risen to touch the face of God! Well done, Reverend Doctor Colonel Robertson. May I someday leave half the legacy upon this earth that you have left.

CONTENTS

Contents

INTRODUCTION

The Church Money Manual is a book unlike any I have ever written. Generally my writing style is to sit down and just write. I go at it frantically day and night for several weeks, roll it all together, and send it to the editor to finalize, bind, and put on shelves. This book came together over a period of years. Some pieces were written over a few days and then nothing would be written for months. I just wrote as I felt a need to communicate something important about finances to the churches I serve. The vast majority of these articles were initially mailed out as newsletter articles to several thousand subscribers who asked Horizons Stewardship, the company I founded, to send it to them. Then we graduated to blog posts on our website.

Regardless of how the articles were distributed, they were practically all done in response to something that had happened to me in the course of speaking to or working with churches. As I heard the question or experienced the issue, it would occur to me that many others might profit from hearing how I responded. So I would return to the office and write about it in a short, to-the-point kind of format. There is very little research data quoted here and only a couple of instances do I reference a book or speaker for an opinion. These pieces are, in most instances, just my answers or ideas on particular issues that I have experienced.

This is real stuff. In these pages you will find comments on debt and the evil that it can be for way too many churches. I'll explore what happens when pastors don't know who the church's donors are and why running around saying that the church is about to die will only expedite said death. You will see pages on why people give and my experiences of what happens when a church ignores those realities. There are stories about capital campaigns, annual campaigns, and planned giving efforts. What does a new pastor do first and second and third upon arriving at a congregation? We'll discuss ways churches can use Easter and Christmas Eve services more effectively, boosting the power and significance of those offering. We'll even examine how to respond to a member who threatens to withhold money from the church unless his or her particular agenda is served or some particular action is taken. The aim here is to cover a wide range of subjects related to money in the church. You may find it quite useful to share particular chapters with members of your leadership team. If you're having trouble shifting a congregant's mind on an issue, maybe I can help. There are no pretend articles in here. Just real stuff!

One preface is necessary. I frequently mention conversations with pastors and tell about something a pastor said or did, and then tell about how I offered a correction. As I read over these articles I am struck by how it appears I am always critical of pastors, always correcting them! Nothing could be further from the truth. I have and always will have enormous admiration for the men and women who serve as spiritual leaders in the 300,000 plus churches in America and many more around the world. Their job is nearly impossible, and yet they keep at it day after day after day. Most of these articles were inspired by a mistake or an issue that was shared with me by the pastor. Since I most often work directly with pastors, it is their stories of both triumph and failure that I draw from here. I have worked with thousands of pastors, and what you will see here is the experiences of only a dozen or so whose stories I believe are instructive for all.

The Church Money Manual, then, is an attempt to help pastors quickly solve some of the common problems that tend to entangle, frustrate, and drain the ministries of the church. It is meant to be accessible, easy to use, and a resource to which you will turn again and again, depending on the situation you face. Ultimately, this book is designed to help you be more effective in your most important work. I think about the pastor who sat up late into the night trying to make the ending of his sermon tie effectively with his introduction because he so fervently believed his people needed to hear it. Or the pastor who left the family dinner table on a holiday because she was notified of another family who was experiencing crisis at the hospital. Or the pastor who stayed on her knees for over an hour with a young couple as their newborn moved ever closer to his last breath. And I think of the pastor who at age ninety-one heard the confession of one of America's top business leaders and then climbed out of his own nursing home bed to baptize the man into new life. This is what pastors do every day, and I am awed and humbled by it. God bless you, servants of the church. I hope this book and all books I write will keep you in the fight to bring our world to Christ.

There is an online appendix to this book that includes samples of resources mentioned in the text. See page 89 for instructions on how to access the online materials.

THE STATE
OF THE CHURCH
AND FINANCE

It Is Not the Economy, Stupid!

In one of Bill Clinton's campaigns, the expression, "It is the economy, stupid!" became very popular. Persons were saying that the reason they would vote a certain way had everything to do with their feelings about the economy. In the last five years, we have certainly heard a number of persons in churches say that their decision about giving would have everything to do with their feelings about the economy. At Horizons, we had to adjust a number of strategies in response to these feelings, which were almost totally negative. For the first time in five years, however, the latest surveys are telling us that the economy is no longer a worry for donors!

In an article printed in the September 26, 2013, issue of *The Chronicle of Philanthropy*, research done by Cygnus Applied Research is cited showing that, in 2009, nearly 60 percent of all donors said they would give less because of the economy. Today that figure is 17 percent.[1] This is certainly good news for all of us who count on donations to fund our mission, but the effects of the recession will be long lasting and in many ways should change the way we do fund-raising in the church and in nonprofits. Below are some of the findings of Cygnus regarding how persons have changed in respect to how they give:

1

75 Percent Now Want to Know Results

Donors now want to make sure their gifts, precious as they are, are getting results! Specifically they say they want to hear from those who have been served, not from paid staff or fund-raisers. They want as intimate a connection to the end product of the donation as they can get. For those of us in the church, this says that donations are more likely to come when donors hear testimony first hand on how the lives of recipients of the church's work have been changed or affected. This part of the study went on to say that donors, now more than ever, want measurable results. How many baptisms, professions of faith, persons in worship, outreach extended? Donors want to measure their impact!

Prompt Thank-You Letters Matter More

We have always known the value of a personal thank-you, and most nonprofits do this fairly well, while most churches do a dismal job. Regardless, 30 percent of those surveyed said that being thanked personally and promptly now matters much more to them than before. This gets back to the point that donors are now much more sensitive with their gifts than before and being appreciated carries more weight. What have you done lately to personally thank your donors?

Young Donors Want to Be Courted

The survey found that young donors are increasing their gifts at a very rapid rate and are experiencing, some for the first time, real income growth. They are trying to make first-time giving decisions yet feel they are being ignored by institutions. They want help in learning about the institution and mission, and they want to be invited to be involved. Many of them even have major gifts to give but are being overlooked. What sort of Christian financial education are you doing? Have you thought of having a "young adults only" session of questions and answers from church leaders?

I am delighted that many persons can see the light at the end of the tunnel from our most recent financial crisis. However, we must learn from this as we move forward. Let's look at a couple of other developments.

IRA Charitable Rollover

The IRA Charitable Rollover, first enacted by Congress in 2006, expired in 2009 and was later reinstated. If the Rollover is in place when you are reading this, (check online or ask a tax accountant, if you're not sure) it is something you should know about and act on. Pastors and finance committees should inform their eligible members of this option because it has gotten very little publicity.

This provision allows individuals aged seventy and a half and older to donate up to $100,000 from their Individual Retirement Accounts (IRAs) to charities without having to count the distributions as taxable income.

Millions of dollars have been given this way by persons who had excess IRA monies. Previously, persons who withdrew these funds for gifts would be penalized by having the money taxed as ordinary income. As in the past, these funds must be directly transferred to the charity, but a donor's IRA administrator and tax advisor will be well aware of how to make that happen.

Pastors, please see that this word is distributed to your congregations. This opens a lot of doors for many of your people to make a year-end gift.

Many persons are rightly concerned about how their cash flow will get them through retirement and, for a few years into that period of life, are reluctant to give substantially. However, once solidly in, a number of them see that they have much more latitude than they realized. Many even see that they have tax issues they didn't have before. Informing seniors of this provision can be a win-win for everyone.

Check with a good CPA or financial advisor and be certain this allowance is still in effect and then get the information to your members who are seventy and over in a clear, understandable way.

Good News: Giving Is Up! (but Not for the Church)

Giving USA, the leading authority on charitable giving, released its findings for 2011. Giving as a whole rose by roughly 4 percent to $298 billion. This is about a 1 percent increase when inflation is factored in. Giving was particularly strong from individuals with bequest giving up by over 12 percent. Giving to health, education, human services, arts, international affairs, environment, and animal organizations were all up. *Giving to religion decreased by nearly 2 percent and is now down to 32 percent of all giving, its lowest level on record.*[2]

The authors of the study wrote, "These [individual giving] increases are encouraging signs of two things: that Americans are feeling better about their personal financial situations...allowing them to continue and even increase their donation levels and that they feel philanthropy remains a core value worthy of support."[3] But what does it say about their feelings regarding the church?

I am not at all surprised that giving increased in 2011. I heard from many donors that they were in much better condition to give that year and had a renewed confidence in what the future would bring. As they chose to give again, or chose to give more, in many instances, they made a decision to leave religion, and specifically the church, out of the equation.

It is interesting that gifts to international charities rose by almost 8 percent. All this money leaves the United States. The local church is right down the block! Persons are saying loudly, it seems to me, that they have far more confidence in these organizations to make a difference in people's lives than they do the missionary efforts of churches. They trust hunger organizations to fight hunger better than their church. They trust educational organizations to fight illiteracy better than their church. They trust health organizations to fight disease better than their church. They trust peace and justice organizations to fight for peace and justice better than their church. Right or wrong opinion, the facts do not lie, and it is abundantly obvious that Americans are losing confidence in the church and distributing their dollars to others to make a difference.

As this piece was being prepared for publication, information was released that showed a continuation of the trend. For 2012, all areas of charitable giving increased except giving to religion. It set a new record for lowest ever percent of giving to religion. Without a sudden reversal and with many churches soon to face a "death tsunami" of seniors dying, the church may soon be in a free fall to calamity. We have a lot of work to do.

4

Capital Campaigns and Building Committees

To Build It Now or Later

I recently visited with one of our area's most prolific contractors. He runs a company that is very active in constructing not only church buildings but also malls, office complexes, and other facilities. He has been in the industry all of his adult life and is an active churchman. I picked his brain, as best as I could, on what was happening in his industry that my churches ought to know. The most important thing he said to me was, "If they need a new facility, they better build now. We are seeing costs rise steadily and do not see an end to it for some time."

I asked him specifically if he felt that a church would be wise to gather up more cash reserves and postpone a project for a year or so. He emphatically said, "Knowing no more than what you just told me, I would say no." I asked him to elaborate on what was going on in the construction industry that caused him to feel this way. Here are some thoughts he shared:

- Fewer companies—The recession caused many people to get out of the construction business, and others decided to stay small. This has created a situation where competition is not nearly as great as before, which causes prices to rise.

- Demand worldwide is high—Large-ticket items like concrete, lumber, steel, and so on are getting worldwide demand. No longer do suppliers only have America to sell to. They can sell their goods all around the world. Demand for goods keeps prices high.

- Skilled labor is not available—During the recession many companies went with inexpensive, often immigrant, workers who could put in cheap hours but had low skills. This caused a number of skilled workers to get out of the trade and do something else. Contractors now have to pay a higher dollar to get the skills they need.

According to this contractor all of the above have caused costs to rise anywhere from 5 to 10 percent in small markets (Little Rock, Topeka, Omaha) and 15 to 20 percent in big markets (Dallas, Houston).

These are facts that any church considering a construction project should add to the equation. What is the price of waiting? In some instances it makes very good sense, but in others, if the enthusiasm and need is there, waiting will only cost you money.

Build It, Then Fund It?

Most of us have heard the phrase "build it, and they will come." This is mistakenly used by persons who want to argue that only if a certain building is built will people flock to the campus to fill it and then, of course, to pay for it. I could provide you with an extremely long list of churches that followed this maxim only to find out that neither the people nor the dollars would come.

Another, not as oft-used but equally dangerous saying is "build it, and then we will raise money to pay for it." This phrase is frequently used by pastors and other church leaders who are in a hurry and want to begin construction before they've offered their congregation a campaign to pay for it.

It all seems quite reasonable to these decision makers. The argument goes like this: "Everyone wants this new building. We have been talking about it for some time. The quicker we do the work, the happier everyone will be. Happy people will be delighted to then pay for what they have, after all God loves a 'cheerful' giver."

The problem is that no one is really thinking like a donor actually thinks. *If you can build something or provide something without me actually having to do something first, it certainly seems to minimize the degree to which you actually need my participation.* You surely cannot say to the donors that unless they give this or that they will not be able to have this or that. You have just taken a building campaign and turned it into a debt campaign. The motivation is totally lost.

The only reason to ever consider turning a spade of dirt or nailing a single board prior to your campaign ending is if there are no other options. For instance, if your roof is leaking horribly and damaging property every time it rains, then time wins out over the campaign and frankly your members would be angry if you did not move rapidly, which would hurt any campaign even more.

The basic rule is do not begin one piece of your project until you have successfully finished the campaign for the project. Not one piece!

Building Committee Mistakes

Recently I met with a new congregation that was about to build its first building. It had grown to 500 in worship and purchased a twenty-acre site. Now the members' attention was on vacating the school they were meeting in and creating their own space. They wanted to have a Q&A session with me one night to talk about all things building finance. The best question of many good ones was, "What are two big mistakes you see made by new congregations, or maybe existing ones as well, that we need to avoid?" I replied that the two biggest mistakes to avoid are most likely to occur at the beginning and at the end of the building process.

First Mistake

The wrong makeup of your building committee will cause delays and frustrating meetings and lead to bad decisions. A church building committee is usually too big and made up of the wrong people. The committee should be between seven to ten persons. Absolutely have no more than ten, whatever size church you are. This will keep meetings from running too long yet still allow for discussion from members. The pastor should be the only staff person who serves as a voting member. Other staff will be in a supportive, consultative role. The committee should be presented as a block for election and not left up to the floor to nominate. The persons should, most importantly, be very knowledgeable representatives of the ministries of the church and be fully committed to the vision for the future. Bankers, contractors, and other professionals are often placed on these committees because of their professions. That is a mistake. The committee's biggest job is *to represent the ministry needs of the church* to the architect, contractor, and bankers it will be working with. Those professionals can do their job better without active interference from other professionals.

Set a time limit on day one of never meeting longer than ninety minutes. If a decision cannot be done in that time, simply bring it up at the next meeting. Building committees make bad decisions when one or two members keep going and just wear the others down. Long meetings also lead to poor attendance going forward, which also leads to poor decisions being made.

Second Mistake

Your eyeballs get too big. Nine times out of ten, and it may be ninety-nine times out of a hundred, the architect will bring back a drawing with a price tag that meets your ministry needs but exceeds your financial capabilities. There is a huge temptation to stretch what should be done because it is "so beautiful and, after all, if we build it they will come!" The problem occurs when, for whatever reason, new people do not come and then you begin a long series of debt campaigns that wears the congregation down and limits your ability to serve in mission and ministry.

The solution is to get extremely good counsel on what your cash flow is liable to look like early on. Hopefully, you will find some creative ways to get your new construction built around the ministry you presently have. If you then find yourself crowded, it is a lot easier to do another campaign for a bit more space than to do it for debt. Many a family starts out in a starter home long before graduating to a larger home that the couple will raise the whole family in over a couple of decades. Churches need to look at initial buildings like a starter home and expect that they will expand it as the church family expands, but will not, metaphorically, build six bedrooms right off the bat before the kids are born.

Many a church would be much better off today if it had formed its initial building committee better and had not let its eyeballs outgrow its wallet.

DEBT

Debt Ratios

I once talked to a United Methodist bishop who was extremely concerned that one of his churches had a debt to budget ratio of 10:1. The budget of the church was around $450,000, and it was carrying a debt of $4.5 million. The church has a beautiful new building that is state of the art, but the bishop's concern and question to me was, "Can this possibly be maintained to where they can do effective ministry and grow the church?" I could not answer him intelligently because I am not privy to the details about the church's ministry, loan agreement, strategic plan, or donor base information. But I could share with him that such a debt ratio alone scares me to death. The interest on this note alone could easily be 50 percent of their entire operating budget. They will have to come up with another $225,000 a year just to pay interest on this loan—which means that none of the $4.5 million in principal will be retired. The national average on a capital campaign for "debt only" is 1.5 times budget. If this church does that, then they will raise exactly enough to just pay interest. If they do two times budget they will retire only about $225,000 in principal and will then owe $4.3 million and face the task of asking the congregation to give an over-and-above gift again and again.

The great fear is that severe donor fatigue will set in and persons will either refuse to keep paying extra and seeing very little for it or leave the church. Remember—the thrill of a new building fades pretty fast and in six years or so it will not look so new, but it will still have the new price tag on it. Families will start to leave, new persons will not see new exciting ministries and thus not join, older members will start to close their checkbooks, and a downward spiral will ensue that might not be stoppable. A church that turns inward to focus on debt is a church that is digging its own grave. Instead of seeking first the kingdom of God, it becomes a church that seeks first to try and pay the mortgage.

My rule of thumb is that a church should not build more than 1.4 times what it raises in its capital campaign. If you raise $1 million then you can build $1.4 million comfortably. Several persons have asked me, "Why so low?" This rule is based on an assumption that you will have a second campaign in three years. In that campaign you want to be able to do one of two things. You want to either be able to say to your congregation that this campaign will "substantially reduce or pay off our debt" or "will pay down our debt while allowing us to add some more space." A campaign that includes needed new space will almost always raise more than one just for debt. Thus, by limiting what you did in the first round, you allow yourself the option of going either way as ministry needs may dictate in the future and you avoid being placed in a corner by your debt. You could even decide that conditions in three years are such that a campaign is not wise and hold off a year with your operating budget covering interest while you wait. In other words, a 1.4 times rule of thumb will allow you options to do what is best for ministry as you move forward. You won't be in a corner with only one option.

The church I reference above has no choice. They must have a campaign. It does not matter if interest rates are 5 or 15 percent, if the community just lost a huge employer or not, if the pastor is good or bad, if the church is growing or shrinking, if we are at war or at peace, or if the stock market is bullish or bearish—they have no choice and that is not where you ever want to be.

P.S. Pastors, don't rely on the fact that people voted for a large expenditure. This will not at all correlate in a few years to their assuming the responsibility to pay for it.

Debt and Capital Campaigns

One day, one of the really solid pastors that I am fortunate enough to work with called me. The conversation went something like this: "Clif, we just got updated numbers from our architect on the building and we are $1.5 million over what we had previously thought. We hit our target on the campaign and have everyone ready to move forward with a vote very soon. I am concerned about where this will put us debt-wise, however, and wanted to run this by you. Do we just add this cost in and borrow more money or do you think we should cut the project back? I don't want debt to come back to hurt our ministry."

I cannot count the number of times I've had this conversation with pastors over the years, except it usually is slightly different because I tend to be told about the increase in amount borrowed after it was already borrowed. I have seen churches wind up borrowing 50 to 100 percent more than was originally projected with no more thought to how they were going to pay it back except that for the next three years they had capital funds to apply. Good business people, wonderful church people, and highly effective pastors are all complicit in the fairy tale that just because it is the church it will somehow get paid back without a problem. What they are doing is exactly what got America in the mortgage mess it has been in the past few years. People found banks that would give them money, so they borrowed the maximum without serious thought about how they would ever pay it back. It has ruined families and it is ruining many of our churches. I can frequently see that a church began to struggle with income and ministry output in direct correlation to when the note rolled around with no solid plan to cover it.

I want all of our churches to step back and think more like Dave Ramsey. As he advocates, we must get off our insatiable belief that credit and debt is the answer. How we spend our money is a spiritual issue with which we are accountable unto God. Is racking up more and more debt really what God is calling your church to do? Do not mishear. I am not anticredit for the church, and I believe that debt can be an effective ministry tool, just like credit can help one buy a house. We just must use far better judgment than we have been using.

Some rules to consider:

1. Don't build more than 140 percent of what you raise in a capital campaign.

2. Have someone do a cash flow analysis showing that you reasonably can be out of debt in seven to eight years.

3. Never let your debt be more than 15 percent of your budget.

4. Never forecast that success demands that you do more than two campaigns back to back.

5. Don't fall prey to "build it, and then they will come." What if they don't?

6. Do calculate start-up/operations cost in your analysis of expenses.

The pastor above and I agreed that he must find a way to cut his project by $1.5 million before going ahead. It would have been easier to sell the idea of adding to the debt, but our projections showed he was maxed out. He made a wise decision. I predict good ministry days ahead for him and his church.

Pastors' Knowledge of Donors and Money

Pastors, Know Your Numbers

In a seminar I hosted one of those in attendance said, "It was brought up in our leadership council meeting that I, as pastor, should have access to all donor information in our church. At first it seemed to be supported but then one man stood and was adamant that doing so would be a great invasion of privacy and I should be denied any knowledge of donor information. His argument won the debate. What do I do?"

I continue to be astounded that this issue is so controversial. Do people not care about their souls? I am a patient at a family practice clinic. I have a doctor assigned to me to help ensure I am physically healthy. When I go to the clinic I am asked to give them some of my blood—privacy invasion! I am asked to remove my clothing so I can be checked for skin cancers—privacy invasion! He looks down my throat and inside my ears and up my nose—privacy invasion! He even asks me questions about my sex life and whether I am having any financial stresses—privacy invasion!

Of course it is all an invasion into my private space, and I can refuse every bit of it, but doing so would put my physical health at risk. Why would I want to do that? I want to be healthy and live a long life playing with my grandchildren. I would be a *fool* not to want my doctor to know everything he or she wants to know. Others also would be foolish and reckless to forbid doctors to do exams they believe are necessary for good health.

Are our souls not worth at least as much as our bodies? Are our pastors not called to be our spiritual advisors and help us safeguard our souls and improve our spiritual health? Should they not sound warnings to us when our souls are in jeopardy? Pastors know that how people give can be a serious indicator of spiritual well-being. Along with other factors they *must* constantly evaluate how those under their care are progressing spiritually. To not do so would be risky to those who rely upon their pastor to help them guard their souls.

If you do not want a doctor to do a thorough exam and to only guess about your health, you are free to pick a doctor who practices like that. If you want a pastor who will just guess about how you are doing spiritually, then you can surely find one. Just do not impose your poor health practice on me by setting up some rule that prevents *my* pastor from truly being *my* pastor. That would be an invasion of *my* privacy!

The Secrecy Sham

It never ceases to amaze me how controversial this issue is in the church. The issue of the leader of an organization knowing absolutely everything he or she can about the revenue stream is a given everywhere but in the church. When asked why, the answer comes back either that the church does not trust the pastor or the pastor cannot trust himself or herself. I wonder why a church would keep a pastor it cannot trust and why a person would chose ministry if he or she does not have self-control?

The question really comes down to whether knowing is better than guessing when one is trying to lead. I have always preferred knowing.

The issue of secrecy is an interesting one. I have never seen a church where a large percentage of income came from cash. It comes from checks, electronic fund transfers (ETF), credit cards, kiosks, or online. The donor's identity then is not secret. It is known by someone—usually several people—in the church. (The question then is who should the people be and whether those people should say thanks to the donors. I have always preferred thanking people to taking them for granted. In forty years of ministry no one has ever gotten mad at me for saying thank you.)

I have frequently heard, "In our church giving is between the giver and God." Really? In your church, doesn't someone count the money and record the gifts? Of course they do. But you say, "They must know the donors' contributions to perform the business of the church." This person is not God!

In your church, do persons not claim their church charitable deductions for taxes? Of course they do, and the accountant records that deduction faithfully. To not do so would not be doing his or her job. This person is not God!

In your church, do persons never seek a loan at the bank and hand over tax returns to the loan officer when doing so? Of course the loan officer must ascertain the financial health of anyone seeking the bank's money. It is his or her job. This person is not God!

A pastor *must* know how people give in order to provide appropriate leadership to the church entrusted into his or her care. A pastor *must* know how people give to help all persons grow in Christ. The pastor is not God. The pastor is just doing his or her job!

More Knowledge = Better Decisions

I was invited to meet with pastors and lay leaders of ten congregations who had great potential but for whatever reason were experiencing difficulties with finances. When it was time for the leaders of one $2 million-budget church to come sit around the conference table, only the pastor presented himself. He said he deliberately chose not to invite any laity until he heard what I had to say first. Well, there was not much I could do about it, so I simply proceeded to review with him the data he had sent and look for issues that needed correcting. Regarding the question of whether he knew who the donors were he replied, "No, I do not. I have been a pastor for thirty years, and I have never found it helpful or necessary. Anyway, I can pretty much guess who they are." Then he said, "But I have read some of your books, and I know you disagree so I asked our treasurer to print out our top fifty donors, and I have the list in an envelope in my coat."

I asked him what he intended to do with the sealed envelope and he said give it to me so I could evaluate the church. I told him it would do me little good but I did want him to open it and look at it himself. He was a bit taken aback, but seeing that no one would witness such a grievous transgression he proceeded to tear open the envelope. Within two seconds he gasped. I inquired into what he saw.

"The second leading donor to my church is a man I hardly know. I see him about once a month when our men's group goes down to the mission to serve dinner, and he always wants to do the dishes. I do not know anything else about him." I pointed out to the pastor that this man was also the second-leading supporter of his ministry. He was not serving on any committee or offering leadership in any arena. He was just giving and washing dishes at the mission. I commented that it seemed that this man might have a genuine relationship with Jesus, but I was not sure. He agreed with a stunned look on his face.

He then got quiet and examined the remainder of the top fifty. At the end of his review he buried his head in his hands and said, "I have a problem. The man I asked to lead our finance and stewardship effort is not in the top fifty. He is the CEO of a Fortune 500 company and has one of the biggest homes in town. I just thought he would be great to head up finance and now I see that he obviously does not get it. What should I do?" Not much he can do at this point. He has asked, and the man has accepted. This pastor has done his church a great disservice by putting the wrong man in charge of the church's pocketbook and failing to lift up another man who just may be a steward others should emulate.

After a few moments of silence the pastor looked up at me and contemplatively said, "I wonder how my ministry might have been different over the last thirty years if I had used this information." We will never know. Let's just hope that he was a good guesser everywhere else.

Large Gifts, Endowments, and Planned Giving

Planned Giving and Endowment Basics

Let this be the year that you form your endowment committee and get them actively marketing for planned gifts (estate gifts). The latest studies out of Boston University continue to document that $41 trillion is going to be transferred from the builder generation to the boomer generation and about half of this will wind up going to a charity. What are you doing to try and get a share of that from your members?

The best time to start planning for these gifts is the beginning of the year. You can systematically lay out a year-long marketing strategy and follow it each week. It is smart and it is good stewardship. Why do we abdicate these gifts to others?

Now do not think that forming a committee will get it done. You must have a solid endowment policy and gift acceptance policy in place. You need a marketing team to plan some seminars, order materials, and do mailings. In short, you need a strategy. (I have put an example in the online appendix of this book.)

One of our clients was relocating. The cost of the new facility was going to be around $12 million. Their budget was $1.2 million and we had to tell them that a capital campaign could not raise what they needed. We predicted and raised $3.5 million. This still left them with too big a gap to do the entire facility so they scaled back and laid plans for a second campaign in three years. They also decided to start their planned giving program. Six months into this marketing plan they got a call from an attorney. One of their members had died and left them $4 million. Immediately, they put the entire project back on the drawing board. Two years later they moved into their new $12 million facility, and after three months we had completed a $4 million campaign to retire their debt.

It does not always happen like this, but if you do not start, I can assure you it will not happen. Let this year be the year you finally take planned giving seriously.

If you hope that this year brings you more resources for ministry, I encourage you to put that hope in the two suggestions above. I think when the year is up you will report that it made a difference. I promise you it won't hurt!

Endowment Policy and Documents

One of our ministry strategists called me to share disturbing news about one of his clients. The pastor had just told him the church was notified that it was the recipient of a multi-million dollar bequest. The pastor was elated, but my strategist was very concerned. He explained that this church, with about a $500,000 budget, was about to go from a position of unity and strength to one of division and weakness. *They had no endowment policy!* He explained that only a few church members knew about the gift, but they were already in divided discussions on how best to use the money. They were preparing for a capital campaign to add on to this growing church and some wanted to cancel that immediately. They had some debt and others wanted to pay that off immediately. There were some others who wanted to place the windfall into an endowment where none of the principal would be used. Then there is the group that felt that all of the money must go to fund missions outside of the church. With just a few people in the know, they had four different ideas of what should be done. This strong church was about to crack because of the wonderful generosity of a recently deceased member. How sad, yet how easily preventable!

If this church had an endowment policy in place, then there would be no discussion. The money would all go to the endowment and be controlled by the policy on exactly how it would be distributed. Good policies use percentages on return as statements on how interest is used. This way the church is protected whether the total in the endowment is a few dollars or millions of dollars. Templates on these policies are available from your denominational foundation or from Horizons Stewardship (horizonsstewardship.com). They are simple and easy (one is included in the online appendix). Policies also can prevent a war in the church and help leadership maintain good stewardship practices from present members while maximizing ministry with the endowment proceeds. Along with a sound endowment policy, every church needs a gift acceptance policy to control what can be accepted and what cannot and under what conditions a gift will be accepted. If you want to see a good fight, let someone offer the pastor their "time share in Florida (that has been for sale for fifteen years while taxes go up!)" and the pastor says no or you accept a nice corner lot that you find out later was a gas station and dry cleaners. After you accepted, it was declared a Superfund Site by the EPA. Guess who is responsible for the environmental cleanup? There goes the new sanctuary.

If your church does not have both of these documents (an endowments policy and a gift acceptance policy) in place right now, then immediately start making arrangements to have them in place within a month. Then when you get millions of dollars you can truly celebrate a wonderful gift instead of worrying if your entire ministry is going to be washed away in a sea of dollars. It may be the first and last time you can say, "We could have had a wonderful ministry there, except we had too much money!"

Avoiding Competition between Planned and Regular Giving

A minister had heard me say that our churches are not nearly as involved in planned giving as they should be and he disagreed.

"I think endowments are a curse upon the church," he started out. "My last church had a substantial endowment and it was the reason I could never develop a sense of stewardship in my people. They did not want to give when they could just use the funds off of someone else's previous gift. It hurt us spiritually in a very significant way. I hate endowments."

This was a message I had heard on numerous other occasions, and I did not doubt for one minute the sincerity of the messenger. He had experienced the horror of a church enslaved by planned gifts. I told him I have a lot of stories where churches have been set free by those same gifts. Endowments can be your master or your servant. It has everything to do with your endowment policy. Too many churches accept gifts and endow them without a policy and this leaves the endowment at the mercy of each year's new crop of leaders. Never begin to promote your desire for planned gifts until you have a comprehensive endowment policy in place.

This policy will state a number of things, not the least of which is that funds from the endowment cannot be used for normal operations of the church. These funds should never replace the annual giving of a congregation but should be used to expand giving. Done right, this policy can actually help you grow giving in your members. Done wrong, just the opposite will occur. My preference for endowment policies is that they restrict undesignated funds initially to maintenance and capital improvements. Churches notoriously let their buildings go until the last minute. Roofs leak for too long. Walls go forever without being painted, and HVAC units live on way past their prime. When these items are dealt with from endowment interest, then persons feel good about their church and often want to give even more for programs that aren't getting rained on or being held in hot rooms. Once these maintenance funds reach a certain percentage of the budget, then the next monies can go for *new* ministries as seed money. These monies are used for a maximum of two years at which time the ministry must be placed within the operating budget.

The policy should also state that *only* interest income can be used. The principle can only be used in cases bordering upon the very survival of the church itself and then only with 90 percent of the leadership body in favor. In other words, it should be locked up pretty darn tight. Any other policies will severely hurt your ability to receive future gifts. At no time should you make the mistake of borrowing from the endowment or "borrowing from ourselves," as I hear expressed. This breaks a trust that you may never get back.

Endowment policies are your key to making endowments your servant rather than your master. Get yours in place right now and then begin to market for those planned gifts this year.

Planning (and Asking) for Legacy Gifts

How many unrestricted gifts of $50,000 or $100,000 did your institution receive last year?

How about $5 million?

In the last five years, The Mint Museum has received *three* bequests of $5 million, due in large part to the work and cultivation efforts of the staff and board members that took place fifteen to twenty years ago during the Ford Foundation Challenge. Fifteen million in five years. That translates to about $750,000 a year in endowment income every year. Forever.

One of the tall steeple churches in Charlotte recently received a $5 million bequest. Up to that point, there had been no active planned giving effort at the church. There is now.

In today's current environment, many nonprofit leaders are struggling to find funding to launch a new program, make up an operating shortfall, increase their reserve fund, or build the capacity of their organization to raise needed funds after having their state and county funding cut.

What many don't appreciate is that the capital for doing all of the above is right under their nose in their current donor base.

Many nonprofit executive directors suffer from the same short-term perspective that plagues public companies that live quarter to quarter to please shareholders. Understandably, directors want the money immediately, so they often insist on hosting galas and silent auctions rather than take the time to visit and talk with their most loyal and generous donors to invite them to consider making a difference forever with a planned gift.

The asking part is important.

According to a donor survey conducted by the Partnership for Philanthropic Planning in 2000, more than 70 percent of the donors who made a planned gift did so because they were asked.[1]

Many nonprofits have policies about using bequests and other planned gifts to build their endowment, but many donors put no such restriction on the endowment. Donors have told me, "If I was worried about how they might use the funds, I wouldn't be giving it to them in the first place."

One of my colleagues shared that when a bequest was recently announced to the session at a Presbyterian church, one of the members said, "I can do that? The church accepts planned gifts?"

Do your donors and members know that your organization is "open for business" and accepts legacy gifts?

Why the Church Must Make Its Case

Our company was fortunate enough to have led a capital campaign for a very large church not too far from where I live. The campaign had gone well and one of the leading donors in that effort made a gift of $300,000, which was a great help to the multi-million dollar campaign. Shortly after this campaign ended, it was announced that this same donor had chosen to give $6 million to his alma mater to help build an art center. I knew the donor well and have great respect for him and his wife so I called and asked if I might come by and have him share with me the process that helped lead to both gifts. He graciously consented.

After I sat down in his lovely home I just got to the point and said, "I simply want to know how you went about determining to give one nonprofit six million and at the same time another three hundred thousand." He understood and began to share.

"First of all, I view all of my charitable donations as investments in changing lives for a better future. I want to feel that what I give is really making a difference. As I became aware of the plans for the center and engaged in conversation with the chancellor, I was convinced that it was the best place for me to put my money and get the return in better lives."

I reminded him that one gift was twenty times that of the other, and he grinned and said he knew that. Then he offered, "Clif, I really love the church, and I want the best for it, but I had to determine with all that I knew about both who would make the best use of the gift. And to me it was not a hard decision at all." I respected that a lot. He is a steward and he genuinely felt that the best stewardship he could make was with a gift to the university. But he had been a member of the church for over thirty years; I wondered how we in the church had failed to convince him.

One interesting fact that he added was that he had a very close relationship with the chancellor. He even noted that the chancellor came by to visit him one week after taking over the university. He talked about their many meetings on strategy and dreams for the school and what a good listener the chancellor was. Then he moved on to how the chancellor came to him with this project, couching it with how he felt this project would really interest my friend. Finally, he directly asked my friend for the $6 million to make the dream a reality.

I asked him if he had any sort of relationship like that with any of his pastors, and he said no. He commented that he had liked all his pastors and considered them friends but that none of them had ever wanted to fully engage him on how he might use his gift of wealth to grow the Kingdom. He said, "You know pastors don't like to talk money very much!" Yes, I know.

I have talked for nearly a decade now about how important it is to help the donors to the church understand how their gifts *change lives*. I have discussed the importance of pastors and church leaders building close relationships with these donors and being willing to ask them for a gift. Seldom, however, have I had it so plainly evidenced as I did on this visit. We simply failed to compete for the best gift. The choice had nothing to do with any lack of money.

We need to pay attention to what my friend is saying and examine how we are relating to our donors. Perhaps we can learn from this conversation so that the next time one of our donors has a choice like this he or she will choose the church.

THE CHURCH'S EXPECTATIONS OF ITS MEMBERS

The Motivation to Give

I recently finished reading Michael Durall's book *Beyond the Collection Plate*. It is an excellent read, and I recommend it to you. As in most things, I liked it because I agree with so much of it.

In the forward, Tom Bandy wrote about what motivates people to give and he said, "The choices postmodern people make to invest their charitable dollars will be determined by the potential to shape their lifestyles around a worthy cause. If the cause is big enough, bold enough, and biblical enough, they will give it everything they have."[1]

He is right on target. The biggest problem I still see in our churches is that we talk way too much about the need for money and not about the ministry being done. We talk about maintaining rather than transforming. We do not help our people to see how they can invest in changing lives but rather how they are supporting an institution. We are afraid to challenge for fear that they will go elsewhere. We keep having annual campaigns to ask for money when persons want more to be a part of a mission. We lower the bar more every year and wonder why we have a church full of couch-potato members.

Recently a senior pastor called me to ask about a staff problem. He had a new associate who did not tithe. The senior pastor wanted to know what to do. He said the young man was very talented and had lots of skills the church needed; however, he had some credit problems and had recently married and tithing was not one of his plans. I asked him if he would excuse the young minister from attending half of the worship services. He said, "Of course not, worship is expected of all leaders!" Why is tithing not expected? Why is a debt to Visa more worthy than a debt to Christ? Giving is not something we do for the church. It is what we do in response to the saving grace that hung on a cross and died for us that we might have life. Tithing is a core value of Christianity, and if we cannot even get our clergy to embrace this principle we have no chance to get the members to.

Be bold! Raise the level of expectations! Believe in your cause and fight for it! Your army of members may not be large, but I guarantee you they will be much more able to fight and to win the spiritual battles that must be confronted in this world.

Are the images of the faith presented in scripture big and bold? Was Jesus hanging on that cross and saying to the thief, "I assure you that today you will be with me in paradise," big and bold (Luke 23:43 CEB)? Was Paul getting on those ships to cross the Mediterranean big and bold? Was Peter standing before the crowds after Pentecost big and bold?

Maybe if our churches would focus more on *big and bold* they would see a few more donations come their way.

Why (and How) to Expect More of Members

An article appeared in the Arkansas Democrat Gazette, the statewide newspaper, about the growth of the Church of Jesus Christ of Latter-day Saints (Mormons). It was a very interesting article that reflected on what the roots of such growth have been when so many other churches are declining. It noted that in the next few years the LDS church will pass The United Methodist Church in population in the United States. Currently they have a little over 6 million members.

I am not a member of the LDS church. I do, however, embrace the way in which they go about their work and how consistent they are in following the tenets of their faith. I have great admiration for the way they do missions, local church work, evangelism, financial stewardship, and the church-wide emphasis they place on family life.

In reading through the article I ran across several comments from the church leaders, who are all volunteers by the way—there is no paid clergy. One was that when they build a new church building it is always paid for before the first worship service. "Mormons don't pass an offering plate on Sundays. Members are expected to tithe, meaning they give 10 percent of their income to the church. We live the law of tithing and we live it strictly. Money for construction, for humanitarian aid, for education all comes from tithing. That is the Lord's money."

The leader went on to say, "Membership comes at a cost. Members are expected to tithe, to attend worship services, to volunteer, and to follow lifestyle rules...The church expects things from their members. When you are a member, you are a member 24/7, even when you are sleeping."[2]

I was struck by how many times the word *expect* was used in the article. Their leadership did not shy away from stating what the expectations of membership were in a very clear fashion. They did not say "proportional giving." They said "tithing." They did not say "serve." They said "two years in missionary service." They don't just say "attend." They say "attend every Sunday."

When you look at your church, what do you see? Are expectations shared unambiguously prior to someone joining or does your church just say, "Come on in, and then we will talk about it"? What do members understand about worship attendance? What are they plainly told about tithing and about mission service or volunteering in the local church? Is there any accountability process?

Examine the expectations of your church. Begin this year to hold classes for prospective members where expectations are boldly laid out and those who are not ready don't join. Could this be the year where you could say, "Membership comes at a cost"? If I read the New Testament correctly, being a disciple of Jesus sure did come with a cost.

LAST-QUARTER PLANNING

Financial Basics for the Next Year

Advent marks the beginning of the Christian year, and we are getting ready for Jesus' birthday party. It is a very special time of the year. Advent should prompt you to begin looking at your financial plans for the next year. What are your plans for financial stewardship for next year? What is the biggest worry you are most likely to have next year? What is it that your members say is not done well at your church? What is the focus of the toughest meetings during the year? What keeps you up at night? In one way or another, for 90 percent of pastors it is money for ministry that keeps them up. It was a struggle this year. It was a struggle last year, and unless you make some real changes it will be a struggle in the year to come. Many pastors will wait until late spring or even summer and then ask somebody in the church to head up a campaign in the fall, during which the pastor will preach on money one Sunday and persons will be asked to once again sign a card. Honestly, right now, do you really think your results will be any different than they have been?

Ask and answer these questions before January is over:

1. *Regarding the annual fund*, when will we have a pledge campaign this year and what will the components be? When will it

be most effective for me to preach about how money affects our lives and why we seem to love money more than we love God? Who are my most generous and faithful donors and how can I uniquely thank them now for what they did last year? When can we start using lay witness testimonies in worship to share how lives have been transformed by Christ and the church? How are we going to effectively communicate our expectation of tithing to our new members this year along with the need to give of their time and talent?

2. *Regarding the capital fund*, what vision are we espousing right now that a capital gift of stock, bonds, property, or inheritance might help us meet? What would we do tomorrow if someone gave us $1 million today? Is that being faithful and bold? If it has been more than five years since any sort of formal campaign was held in our church, what can we do to encourage these gifts to come to us rather than another nonprofit?

3. *Regarding the endowed fund*, are we prepared with policies and procedures for planned gifts? What will be our marketing strategy for planned gifts this year? Do we know today what we will be doing ten months from now to encourage these gifts? When will we start asking each person to put a tithe in his or her will for the church?

Yes, my friends, Easter will come along again next year. Christmas will also be held again. It is possible, however, that your regular headaches over financial stewardship could go away with a bit of planning now. You might even find that you and your members enjoy Easter and Christmas a whole lot more when giving is more up than down.

New Year's Resolutions for Every Year

A lot of my pastor friends find themselves consistently trying to keep the bills paid and members happy while watching the ushers pass lighter and lighter offering plates, year after year. A lot of them spend much of their time around Christmas e-mailing or frantically calling to try and salvage something in the year-end budget. I offer these New Year's resolutions for pastors who would like to get a more positive result. These are not just for the start of a new year, of course. These are tactics and strategies that will improve your results at any time.

None of these resolutions will replace having a church that is changing lives with ministry that is meeting real needs in a real world, but adopting some of these recommendations should help give you a better outcome than last year.

I will thank people personally. This needs to be the year that you start writing those ten personal thank-you notes each week, taking one major donor to lunch a week, and making one appreciation call a day. A friend of mine, who is a pastor, wrote me at the end of the year to share the difference his thank-you notes were making. He writes a letter to each family the first time they give and sends them a copy of *Fields of Gold.* This reinforces the importance that the church and pastor place on generosity and opens up a dialogue about giving early on in the year. It took some time at first, but Jim did not have to send out emergency letters in December.

I will get serious about planned giving. This should be the year that you get your endowment committee to do a year-round job of marketing for planned gifts for your endowment. At a minimum, make it your goal to grow an endowment equal to five times your budget. Draw up a plan as to what will be done each quarter to promote the advantages of planned gifts for the donor and for the church. As the pastor you should personally *ask* one potential donor each month to consider a gift (if your attendance is more than two hundred). If you will spend fifteen hours getting this started early on in the year, you will not have to spend fifteen hours the entire rest of the year on it.

I will preach on giving and generosity in January and in September. One of the constants that I continue to see is excellent per capita giving in churches where the members tell me that their pastor boldly and consistently preaches about tithing and generosity. It is also true that in the churches where I get asked to help them grow in giving, the members report to me that they seldom hear a sermon on giving until the church is begging for more.

I will joyfully tithe. Giving is such a joy and brings so many blessings to our lives. If you have been afraid of that joy, this is the year to experience it. If it is, indeed, a new faith venture for you, then confess it to your members and ask them to pray for you and to join you on the journey. One of the greatest and most effective sermons I ever heard was from a pastor who confessed his sin of "loving things too much." He said he wanted a more fulfilled life and was going to trust God with all. At the end of the service, it was like an AA meeting: one member after another joined the pastor in the confession and committed to a new life of generosity.

A Strategy to Increase Year-End Giving

At the end of the year, church leaders look at income and consider how best to communicate with their congregations about why and how to give more. A similar concern is heard in all the radio chatter about football coaches and whether they will be retained or not at the end of the year. I once heard a college football analyst discussing a certain coach and the decision the school was going to have to make. He said, "Look, there will be lots of discussion on both sides, but it will come down to wins and losses. There just have not been enough victories. He is winless in the conference and has not beaten the key rival in four years. Yes, the program has been free of major scandal. Yes, he is a good man with a fine family. From all accounts he works hard and with integrity, but he has not made an impact on wins and losses. Ultimately, persons are going to fill the stands, spend money on the program, and give more scholarships when they see impact and victories. He has not convinced them. I imagine he will go."

I would suggest to you that church people think much the same way. You can have a very nice person ask for support. You can tell people you have bills to pay. You can say that the church has been open for business each and every day, but ultimately support will be dependent upon victories. Church support comes when people see that they got results from their investment. If it is a result they highly value, then they will give more support. But they want victories. They want to see the victory of persons baptized at the altar. They want to hear the victory of a drug-dependent person sharing how Christ set him or her free. They want to experience the victory of a child drinking from a clean water source for the first time. They want to experience the exhilaration of the Spirit as worship takes them to a new level in their relationship with Jesus. You give them victories, and they will give you support. You keep running up losing seasons, and all the begging at the end of the year will go for naught. Money really is not the problem—it comes down to wins and losses.

This year as you prepare to write that end-of-the-year letter, remind members of the victories the church had this year. Put the stories in first person as often as you can ("added ten people to the roll" is not an impact victory!). Instead of telling them you are a few thousand dollars behind, just put half a dozen testimonies on two pages where people share the victory they found in Jesus, and close with a note saying thanks for helping change lives. Then note that you want to change twice that many next year. The support will flow your way.

Think about it. Why do Alabama, LSU, USC, and Oklahoma have a lot more money and fans for football than Utah State, Indiana, New Mexico, and Rice? People fund winners both on the football field and in the church house. Did you have more wins than losses this year?

Doom-Saying

Why Doom-Saying Does Not Work

The letters have started.

"As we approach the year's end, we are not going to be able to pay our denominational support fund (change name to suit). We hope everyone remembers that they vowed to support the church when they joined and will examine their giving for the year."

"As we move into Christmas, let us all be aware of the gift that came in the manger and consider what gift we should be making to the church. We don't want to finish in the red again this year like last year."

"We have done about all we can do to cut expenses at the church. Your staff has cut back on programming to the bare minimum. Now we need you to increase your giving to keep us solvent through Christmas."

The above are examples of what is being sent out by churches all over America. They are similar to letters that went out last year and the year before that. The basic message is "you owe me." They are cries of desperation and pleas for cash as everyone sings "Joy to the World." You wonder why persons think they can continue to do the same thing year after year and yet somehow get a different result this year.

Let's stop the madness of crying and begging every Christmas and start doing real life-changing ministry all year long. Donors are telling us more and more that they are becoming more sophisticated and discriminating with the charities they will support, but the church still seems to ignore the warnings.

Advancing Philanthropy reported that the Cygnus Donor Survey has once again asked America's donors what organizations they will most likely support, and they got the same answer this year they have gotten for the last twelve years. Seventy-three percent of the respondents said they favor giving to nonprofits that provide them with "measurable results on what has been or is being achieved with donors' contributions."[1] At the same time they found that failure to receive measurable results on their gifts remains the number one reason they stop giving or give less than they could.

I worked with a church that spends $250,000 for every convert, a person joining on initial profession of faith. This church does not need to purchase a different stewardship program for next year; they need to start bringing people into a relationship with Christ. When they start doing that, persons will witness it and begin giving them more money to do more of it.

Perhaps our push this Advent season should not be to make certain we finish in the black with money but with converts. Perhaps our denominational leaders who make those calls to their pastors each December asking, "Will you pay out?" should instead call and ask what they are doing to win someone to Jesus in the last month of the year. The majority of persons who give money to the church really do want to see Jesus' work being done, not the budget balanced.

What are your specific plans for reshaping evangelism next year? How will you share testimonies? How will your donors hear about lives being changed? How will success be measured?

Once again, America's churches will have a smaller percentage of persons in them than the year before. Once again we will see that donors are choosing to give less of their income to the church than the previous year. Do we love Jesus enough to ensure that next year will not see a continuation of this trend?

Helpful Alternatives to Doom and Gloom

I was in a worship service and the pastor turned the microphone over to the finance chairman, who gave what has become a routine report on the condition of the church as it approached the Christmas season. "We are substantially behind our budget projections," he said, "and I fear that without many of you making some extra gifts to the church we will not be able to meet our obligations." He went on to spell out some of the numbers, but they all seemed blurred to me, and I began to shut him out. I had heard such a plea perhaps a hundred times over the years and each one sounds like the ship is sinking. I began to ask myself, "How stupid am I to keep getting on a ship that every year they tell me is about to sink? I need to find a better ship."

I know that most of you reading this will find yourself in a position of deficit as you approach the last few weeks of the year. Take heart—most churches in America are in the same boat. December has generally been the highest giving month of the year for a vast majority of our churches. It will be again this year. We are not helping ourselves or improving the quality of worship to keep inserting these talks right as much of America is coming to us for Thanksgiving and Christmas. We will have thousands come into our churches at this time of the year who have not been there since Christmas last year. We have a chance to carry the good news to them, and instead we substitute a financial report. Here is what I suggest:

If you absolutely must communicate the church's financial condition to the membership, then do it in a private letter or e-mail and keep it away from those who may be coming to you to experience the joys of Thanksgiving or the birth of the Christ child. If persons can leave your church and truly feel that they found spiritual nourishment and enrichment, they will come back, and they might become contributors. If, however, they come and feel that they are fleeced right off the bat, they will not want to repeat that experience.

Put together a wish list for Christmas for the church and place it in the pews, in the narthex, on the website, or in the bulletin. Say something like, "For those wishing to truly give Christ a gift on his birthday, here are some things that his church, his body, could use this year and next," and then give an extensive list. This can include some things that you may be including in your budget and not just extras. Make it diverse. For instance, you can list "Pay for VBS

$_____, Buy a crib for the nursery $_____, Send one child to church camp $_____, Buy a Church Van $_____." Have a list of thirty or forty things and, as they get chosen, mark them off the list for the next week.

People like to designate. They have extra money at the end of the year. You need items for your church. It is a win-win. But how does it help with your denominational obligations? If members will buy things that are in the budget with this money, you will have more regular offering available for the other things. And everyone will feel good about it and not beat-up.

Mike Slaughter wrote a fabulous book called *Christmas Is Not Your Birthday*, which details how his congregation gives at Christmas. Each member is asked to give to a specific mission effort an amount equal to what they will spend during Christmas. It has been a phenomenal success. Mike did not want his family or his church family to forego the joy of exchanging gifts and love during Christmas. He just wanted all to remember whose birthday it really is. The result: they raised hundreds of thousands of dollars for mission and have raised members' spiritual relationship with Christ. That is what Christmas is for.

THE POWER OF PURPOSE

Be Impactful

I was at a church recently meeting with a rather large group of supporters. During the meeting a young woman asked to speak, and I sure am glad she did. She said,

> I came this afternoon to thank all of you for what you did two years ago in making the new children's wing a reality. I know that many of you do not have children at home anymore, but I do, and this new facility has been a godsend for our family. We had been struggling with our youngest child. She was new at her school, and no children lived in our neighborhood. We were watching her grow increasingly inward and just not seeming to like herself very much.
>
> One Sunday morning we decided to come here to church even though neither my husband nor I were active churchgoers growing up. We had just watched the new wing being constructed and thought it would not hurt to try it out. My husband said that there was no football on that afternoon anyway. Well, we came a year ago and obviously we have not left. On that first Sunday my daughter was greeted by Miss Susie and welcomed by other children. She was mesmerized by the computer stations and interactive Bible games. The children's music time actually got her singing, and we hear those songs around the clock now in our

home. I am ashamed to say she was the one who got us to start praying before meals.

Well, not only was it a godsend for her but for my husband and me, too. Since we were bringing her we had to find a place for ourselves, and we landed in the Genesis Class where we actually found some people who did not know much more about the Bible than we did, but were trying to learn. Tim got into Habitat with some of the guys, and I have found new life in my women's small group. We now know Jesus Christ as our personal Savior and not just as a historical figure.

None of this would have happened if those of you in this room had not done what you did for people like us who you had not even met yet. You have changed our lives and our family. From the bottom of my heart, thank you.

IMPACT! Every donor in that room now knew exactly what the impact of their generosity had been. This one story meant so much more than some shared statistic like "since we built the space we have twice the number of children as before."

This story, and not a statistic, will bless the hearts and the wallets of all who hear it. Are you sharing your stories? Are you helping persons to feel in their heart what sort of impact their generosity is having? This year, focus on impact and every Sunday consider how you can help persons know they are having an impact on lives! If you cannot think of any testimonies, then you have other issues to deal with.

Why Cool Doesn't Rule

A few years ago I was talking with a top Wal-Mart executive. I voiced to him that I felt they needed a new store at a certain location because the present one was not as cool looking as some of the new ones. He grinned at me and said,

We are not in the "being cool" business. We are in business to make a profit and grow shareholder value. That is what we do and why we exist. The store you reference is highly profitable and able to serve our customer quite well. When we see that it is not going to be so or that a new one will readily produce more profit, we will build. Until then, we are happy.

I have also witnessed the opposite by businesses. Just today I was reading about a prominent businessman whose lifetime of assets is being auctioned off for inability to make payments. He had a very profitable business, and he used it to look cool. He had his own private jet and hangar. He had several houses in a row. He had a magnificent horse farm and threw lavish parties for the whole community. Now he is broke! What a tragedy.

Which one of these attitudes best describes your church? Too often I see good churches start making decisions to look cool when they are in the building process. They begin to do things that have no real relationship to their mission, but it looks cool. No one seems to be looking at the bottom line. In working with troubled churches, I see a common pattern. The decline began when they overbuilt and overborrowed.

The question to be asked is, "Will this investment improve our bottom line and, if so, to what extent?" The bottom line for churches is disciples for Jesus Christ! This should be how we measure any investment as a church. The return is in new lives for Christ. So how many more disciples will be made by putting computers in every classroom? How many more disciples will be made by having rocking auditorium seats versus straight back? How many more disciples will be made by having offices that are 20 x 20 versus 10 x 15? How many more disciples will be made by using brick all around versus just a brick front? Does the elevator need mahogany paneling, or will wallboard make just as many disciples?

I am not arguing that our churches need to look cheap or be poorly made. Not at all. I am arguing that we must remember our mission and remember that good stewardship means always doing as we feel the Master would have us do. He said clearly, "Seek first the kingdom of God....Go therefore and make disciples!" (Matthew 6:33; 28:19 NKJV). This is the mission. It is the sole reason we should do whatever we do. If you are in a building process, is this the primary question guiding all discussion? It should be!

Easter as an Opportunity for Purpose-Based Giving

Easter is the greatest celebration in the Christian year. It is a time to shout, sing, and rejoice that our Lord and Savior, Jesus Christ, rose from the grave to live forever and ever. Christ the Lord is risen! Now please pass the plate.

I am quite often asked about why giving on Easter Sunday is lower than the church expected it to be. After all, for most churches more people will be in worship this day than any other Sunday of the year. Many a finance committee has said to me that it was waiting for the Easter offering or holding out to see what comes in at Easter or something like that. They believe persons give a lot on that day. They look at church like a store. On days when there are more customers, there are usually more sales and higher receipts. This is, however, not a good analogy when it comes to giving and the church. In fact, if you wanted to measure per capita giving, you might find that Easter was one of the lowest Sundays for giving per worshipper during the year. The reason is really quite simple, but one that pastors and laity never seem to quite understand.

Persons who truly love Jesus give. Those who do not love Jesus usually do not give. Persons who truly love Jesus as their Lord and Savior are in church most every Sunday of the year and do not wait around for Easter to show up. People who only come on Easter will drop a dollar or two in the plate, but they do not have the church prioritized for a large gift. They have come for pageantry, special music, fellowship, tradition, family gathering, or some other reason. Their attendance seldom has anything to do with the joy that Christ arose. These persons will pay something for admission to the event, but will not usually make any real commitment or contribution.

Now, I do not want to minimize the fact that these persons are there. I am thrilled that they have come to be exposed to the gospel. We should rejoice in that, but do not expect a spike in attendance to produce lots of funds for the rest of the year, unless the gospel truly takes root.

But, you say, can't we do something to get their wallets to loosen up a bit? Yes, you can. You can have a special offering envelope prepared for persons to use to make a gift to a mission opportunity like feeding the hungry at the downtown mission or building a Habitat home or repairing an inner-city school playground. It must be something outside of the church. Tell persons that 100 percent of the funds in those envelopes will go to this project. Show a short video of the need and how the church can help. Share how this is an expression of the risen Christ at work in their lives. This offering is taken up at the same time as the regular offering, but the envelopes will separate the funds.

You will find that visitors or infrequent attenders will like the idea of giving to something like this. They will give considerably more to this than they would to "the church." The fund-raising will not interrupt your service but actually add a wonderful mission component to what is done that day. This will not necessarily help your operating budget directly, but it will take money out of persons' pockets to serve God's least and lost, and I bet that is a better use for the money than what those persons were going to use it for.

You can follow this model during Christmas Eve or any other Sunday when you will have a substantial number of nonmembers or nominal members present.

Christ is risen; he is risen indeed!

Why Are We Here?

In an earlier chapter, I shared a story of a very active church member who had just chosen to give a multi-million dollar gift to his college and a much smaller donation to his church. In visiting with the donor, whom I have known for years, he commented that he just felt that the college would be able to do more with it to "impact lives." I understood and appreciated his candor. I told this story in a seminar I led recently. My sharing of the story was done to say that if we want such gifts we have to be ready to share how we "impact lives."

I got a quick rebuttal from a senior pastor who said, "How can we expect to have the impact of a college? They have thousands of students and huge budgets. We simply cannot compete with that!" I was stunned and for a few seconds did not know how to respond to a pastor who was throwing up a white flag without even firing a shot. It was depressing, but I imagine all too real.

How important is what we do in the church? What is the value of one soul? Do we really have something to offer that a college cannot duplicate? Would the world miss us if we were not here?

I am afraid that this pastor and many others simply do not know the mission. He computes that since a college has more persons than his church, they can have more influence and more impact. The education of one student to be a sound businessperson or a school-teacher holds equal or more value than leading someone to know Jesus Christ as their Lord and Savior. The college can make more people "good people" than the church.

My friends, I value my college and what it did for me. I value the contribution that many nonprofits, like Boy Scouts and Hospice, have made to my life. However, nothing has made the difference that having a relationship with Jesus Christ has made and, yes, I do think it really matters! I am willing to put the case of a healthy and fruitful church over anything on the planet. Do our church leaders not believe that anymore?

Untapped Potential for Positive Change

Recently my friend sent me an article from the *Orange County Register* written by Cathleen Falsani. In her article she referenced a talk done recently by Richard Stearns, who is the CEO of World Vision. In his outstanding talk he noted how "Christians" (he did not even count non-Christian people) could truly change the world in a very short time. Here are a few snippets that I have paraphrased from what he said:

In the United States there are 350,000 churches and 238 million individuals who self-identify as Christians.

These Christians average giving 2.4 percent of their income away. The vast majority of this goes to churches.

This amounts to about $125 billion per year.

What if these same Christians elevated their giving by just 1 percent?

This would amount to an extra $52 billion a year.

Over twenty years this amounts to a bit over *one trillion dollars* *($1,000,000,000,000).*

It is estimated that clean, safe water can be provided to every person on the planet for about $70 billion. By doing that we could seriously reduce child mortality and illness, free up parents for productive work, and change rural communities forever. *We can do that!*

The UN estimates that it will take $300 billion to eliminate malnutrition on the planet. *We can do that!*

We have $670 billion left.

For $86 billion we can wipe out malaria. *We can do that!*

For $30 billion we can make microloans to 100 million potential entrepreneurs, creating 250 million jobs. *We can do that!*

We have taken care of food, water, and disease, and employed 250 million people. We have decimated extreme poverty and human suffering, and we have $454 billion left.[1]

I would add these to the list:

Let's plant thousands of new churches all over the world for $100 billion. *We can do that!*

Let's build a new modern hospital in every third world country and supply them with trained physicians who will teach and train native physicians and nurses for $200 billion. *We can do that!*

We could build 25 million homes for those who have no shelter for $254 billion. *We can do that!*

This is just ridiculous, isn't it? It is as crazy as hearing that someday the lamb will lie down with the lion or that there will someday be a place where there are no more tears. Stupid stuff! But it is not ridiculous to those who are suffering, starving, thirsty, and without a home.

It is not ridiculous or stupid at all. It is just 1 percent. We can do that!

Setting the Budget on Purpose

When I started out in ministry nearly thirty-five years ago, I wandered into my first church board meeting with wide eyes and my mouth firmly shut. I did not know much about running a church business meeting. None of my theology or Bible classes dealt with that. I watched as the first report was called for. It was the report from the finance committee. The chairman handed out a line item budget and went over the status of the church. If the budget was balanced then everyone seemed to be happy. If it was not, then there was considerable consternation and demands for what were we going to do about it. All the other reports were secondary to this one. To a young neophyte it was very clear as to what the priority was: balance the budget. I even discovered in many instances this was also the priority of my superiors in the church. If I got my connectional obligations paid, then I was doing a good job in ministry. One learns early on what is required and how to succeed, and the message was brought home to me that finances were the key to the kingdom.

Since that time, I have been a part of church leadership meetings from Baptist congregational gatherings to Presbyterian sessions to Methodist councils. Consistently I still see that the first report often given is from the finance committee and that seems to be the one that most persons want to discuss (or argue over as the case may be). I have especially watched in the last two years as many churches have focused like laser beams on what is happening with their internal finances. Personnel and programs have been slashed, sometimes not because of a lack of money but because of fear of impending doom.

Now I do not want to be misunderstood and for anyone to think that we should never see how we are managing our money or that we do not need to be good stewards of every dollar that is given to the church. It just should not be the center focus of our church lives. Nowhere do I see in the Bible that balancing a budget should be our concentration. It even appeared that Judas was resolutely criticized by Christ for doing just that when Mary was anointing him with oil. Judas's eyes were on the checkbook and Jesus said they should be on him.

We should start our business meetings with how we are doing with why we are in business—our purpose. What have we been doing since our last meeting to make disciples of Jesus Christ? How many new converts have we won for the Kingdom? What evidence do we have that persons are growing in their relationship with Christ as a result of what we are doing? Have we grown in the number of persons who are coming to worship, involved in learning opportunities, or committed to giving their life away in missions?

If Boeing concentrates on making better airplanes than Airbus, they will sell more planes and make more money. If General Motors concentrates on making better cars than Toyota, they will sell more cars and make more money. If McDonald's concentrates on making a better burger than Wendy's, they will sell more burgers and make more money. If any of these concentrate as a first priority the making of money, they will eventually be out of business.

One of the best things you can do to raise more money for your church is to give evidence to your donors that you are focused on why you are in business—making disciples—as a first and only priority. You do that well, and the budget will take care of itself.

TITHING AND HOW TO LEAD IT

The Ninety-Day Tithing Challenge

There is not a single major denomination that does not encourage tithing by its membership. Strong statements are in place from Catholics to Pentecostals. Yet we see that far less than 10 percent of the church members in America practice this level of generosity. In mainline denominations the number of tithers is closer to 2 percent. There is nothing I have ever found to increase one's relationship with God more than learning to part with that which persons love more than God. Putting an emphasis on tithing should do exactly that. It should never be about getting more money but always be about helping persons grow to trust God more. It will be that trust that brings them ultimate joy and fulfillment, not the money they were previously relying on. To have a more Christ-focused congregation, conduct a ninety-day tithing challenge for April, May, and June. Beginning early will allow you to get books ordered and get your staff ready. Here's a plan, part of which I learned from Nelson Searcy of Journey Church as noted in the book *Maximize*:[1]

1. Two weeks prior to the challenge starting, the pastor must preach on his or her tithing experience and how that spiritual discipline has influenced his or her life. It is also important

that at this time *all* staff have agreed to participate in the challenge.

2. Continue with a second sermon on tithing and issue a challenge that all families of the church tithe for ninety days beginning the first Sunday in April. Have a commitment card handy in the pews or chairs for persons to sign right then and hand in. The next day send an e-mail to all members sharing about the challenge and give those not present a chance to e-mail in and take the challenge.

Ninety-Day Tithing Challenge   April 1 – June 3

I accept the challenge to:

-Tithe (give 10 percent of my gross income) to my church for the next ninety days

-Pray for the Lord to bless my church and use me faithfully within the church for the next ninety days

-Read ninety chapters of the New Testament over ninety days

Signed: _____

---

3. By Tuesday or Wednesday send a personal letter to each family who took the challenge and enclose a gift of either *Treasure Principle* by Randy Alcorn, *Fields of Gold* by Andy Stanley, *Money Matters* by Mike Slaughter, or *Enough* by Adam Hamilton. The letter should express thanks and offer encouragement. Do not neglect this important follow-up step.

4. The following Sunday share the number of persons who accepted the challenge, and let persons know they will be hearing testimonies from various ones as you go through the ninety days. Beginning on the first Sunday in May, start a weekly (three-minute) testimony from someone who accepted the challenge. The rest of the service can deal with any topic you desire.

5. In the middle of May, send another letter to those who accepted the challenge, letting them know you are continuing to pray for them and wanting to hear from them about their experience and how it is affecting their spiritual lives.

6. One week before the ninety days ends, send another letter thanking all those who took the challenge and asking those who felt it helped them grow spiritually if they were going to continue with the discipline or cease. Give them another card to respond to what their intentions are going forward as well as an e-mail address, if they want to respond that way, and then publish the results the following week along with sharing them in worship. Be sure and keep good records of those signing up.

Where Am I Going from Here?

Following the ninety-day challenge I intend to:

-Continue with the spiritual disciplines of the ninety days (tithing, praying, reading)

-Continue with parts of the disciplines:

_____

-Go back to my old life

Signed: _____

Three things will be very important to being successful: First, the pastor must practice all the disciplines and very specifically testify to it. Second, the emphasis must be on the spiritual benefit and never the monetary benefit to the church. Third, the follow-up contacts must be made throughout the ninety days.

I will be anxious to hear how this works out for you. I believe it will. Following this you can have a ninety-day mission challenge or a ninety-day worship attendance challenge or a ninety-day fill-in-blank challenge. Perhaps all will lead to lifelong change and the making of disciples.

Your Tithe *and* Your Heart

The other day I visited a young man who is a "Little" in the Big Brothers Big Sisters program. He was telling me about his father who lived in another city but one not too far away. The boy said that his dad faithfully sends a check in for his child support and will buy him a birthday and Christmas present but rarely expresses a desire to be with him. As he spoke you could see the hurt in his eyes and on his face. He said that even in the summer when he goes to see his dad that the father is often very busy and sends him off to a cousin or family friend. It was great to get the money, but more than anything the boy wanted the love. He wanted a relationship with his father that his father obviously did not want.

Not long after that I found myself talking with a woman who was very angry with her ex-husband for calling their child and talking a lot with the child and wanting to come be with the child but not paying child support or purchasing school supplies. She said, "He thinks withholding the money is just hurting me and not his son, but it is hurting his son. I cannot buy him all the things he needs for school or even to get dressed properly. The attention is nice but it is hollow without something behind it for groceries and all."

All of this got me thinking about how I feel about tithing. I have been a longtime tither, giving God at least 10 percent of what I earned, and on occasion I have lapsed into thinking that now that I have tithed I can just do with the rest of my money exactly as I please. I have also known a number of persons who wanted to trade tithing for time assuming that God had some sort of point system and that they would get enough from one area to substitute for another.

I found myself remembering Matthew 23:23 where Jesus said, to paraphrase, "you tithe, but…" Jesus was not saying that giving the tithe was bad. Not at all. He was saying that only giving the tithe and not loving God or loving our neighbor was to totally miss the point. It was not our money that Jesus was after, but a relationship. He was saying that God wants us to be in a loving relationship with him more than anything else. Tithing is and should be one part of that expression of love. I should not want to tithe so I will get something in return. I should want to tithe because of the simple fact that I love God and am so grateful for all God has done for me.

A father who says he wants to have a relationship with a child but refuses to share a portion of his wealth with him or her is not a father who truly loves his child. A father, on the other hand, who only sends his child money, no matter how much, but does not desire to spend time with him or her, is not a father who loves his child. Both reflect a person who is too much in love with himself and those things he values more than a loving relationship—money or time.

Tithing is important to me, and it is necessary for me. Not so I get points or will go to heaven. It is necessary for me to have and sustain a loving relationship with my heavenly Father.

HELP FOR THE HARD TIMES

What to Do If First-Quarter Giving Is Down

The pastor of a church Horizons led a campaign for a couple of years ago and I talk quite often about a number of things, not the least of which is his church and the progress that is being made in various ministry areas. This church has shown some exciting growth in a number of areas and usually our visits are celebratory. One day he called me and was a bit distressed. For the first quarter of the year, giving to church operations was down from the previous year. He asked if he could send me a letter to review that he was considering sending to the congregation about the shortfall.

When I am asked about issues like this my first questions are research ones. Exactly how much are you down from the same time period last year and the year before? How much are you off your budget projections? Are there any obvious reasons for the shortfall like heavy snow Sundays or did you even have the same number of Sundays last quarter? What is going on with worship attendance? Are there any conflicts in the church that may be causing some reaction? All these questions and more need to be answered prior to any letter being sent.

The biggest question to answer, however, is what is going on with your top ten or twenty donors. They are probably responsible for a big percentage of the budget. I remember one pastor who called me and then e-mailed me a lengthy letter he was sending to all of his members to encourage them to increase their giving because the church was unexpectedly behind by $50,000 early in the year. He was alarmed because if he prorated that out it meant a $200,000 shortfall on the year. He wanted to jump right on it. I encouraged him to review the donor list, which he had never done and was reluctant to do. When he did he saw that one donor who always gave a January check of around $35,000 had paid nothing. One phone call reassured him that the check was soon to be sent and the donor was sorry he was a couple of months late on his usual contribution date. Suddenly, things did not seem so dire. The pastor realized it was not his entire membership that was decreasing their giving. Most of the shortfall lay in one individual who was a bit late on his normal schedule. A strongly worded letter encouraging persons to help their "distressed" church would have been a bad idea and possibly even backfired on the preacher.

When my pastor friend called, I asked him if he knew what his top donors were doing, and he confessed that he did not and would check this out thoroughly before drafting any letter.

Could the treasurer do this and just report findings to the pastor? Yes, but it is not nearly as effective. It is assumed that the pastor knows his or her congregation better than anyone else. Are contributions down from someone because of a death or divorce or job loss or other crisis that a treasurer would not know about? Treasurers are treasurers because they do numbers well. Pastors are pastors because they know numbers reveal things that are personal and soulful. The church needs the pastor's heart to help interpret numbers appropriately.

Times of Trial

Donors are cutting back on giving to churches and nonprofits in a serious way. A recent Barna research study shows some trends that do not bode well for church or nonprofit giving. Barna reports that nearly half of all adults (48 percent) say they reduced their nonprofit organization giving in the last quarter of 2009. Twenty-nine percent reported that they had reduced giving to their church. When the recessionary crisis first hit in the last quarter of 2008, about 10 percent of Americans said they had to cut back their church giving by at least 20 percent. At the time of the study, the report says nearly 25 percent of churchgoers have cut back their individual contributions by at least 20 percent. All in all, Barna reports that giving to churches in 2009 dropped by about 7 percent and 2010 didn't look any better.

One very interesting side note was that the number of tithers has *not* gone down. About 7 percent of all adults report giving at least 10 percent of their income to a church or nonprofit. This figure has not decreased in the economic crisis. Evangelicals far outdistanced all other religious groups in the number of self-identified tithers.[1] This helps explain what I have seen in many of the churches we work with. In those churches where persons have a real passion for sharing the gospel and Sunday morning is a genuine celebration of new life, hope, and resurrection, the congregation continues to thrive with new people and new money regardless of what is happening in the community economically. They just seem to want to give!

Now some will read the above and say, "Well, I sure feel better knowing that my church is not the only one suffering a downturn. As long as my suffering is shared by others, it just does not hurt as much." Others of you, I hope, will say, "In light of this, what must I do to garner support for my church and achieve maximum generosity?" Let me offer some suggestions for when you are in times of trial.

1. Don't panic. God is still sovereign. *If* you are living in the midst of God's will and doing God's work, you will be blessed. Have faith in God to be your partner.

2. Tell your stories. Redouble your efforts to tell life-changing stories. People still have money and they will give, but they are much more discriminatory. They want to know that good things are happening with their donations.

3. Serve. Create ministries and programs to assist persons in financial crises. Start job counseling services, teach résumé classes, and offer free babysitting while parents job hunt. Host a job fair and communicate the pastor's willingness to counsel. Never send the message that you are a church that only wants to be on the receiving end. Be a giver.

4. Preach, preach, and preach on the role of money in our lives. Some persons are just now coming to the realization that money will not save them. They are more open to sermons on money today than ever before.

5. Talk to donors. Yes, your people are donors and not just members. More than likely your budget is heavily supported by ten to twenty families. Go see each one. Thank them for their giving and ask them what their plans are for the year. Businesses all over America are contacting their best customers directly and asking them about future plans. You should do the same. Don't guess!

6. Start a study series using books that deal with money and giving in our lives. Two I like are *Fields of Gold* by Andy Stanley and *Enough* by Adam Hamilton. Help persons dialogue about money and faith. We have kept money in the same closet as sex in the church, and it has hurt our people spiritually for too long.

7. Hold financial management classes. If you have not begun using Financial Peace University or Crown Ministries as tools to assist your people in managing their money, start right now and keep going all year long with one after the other. Your people need these practical tools to get control of their financial lives.

You have two choices in these difficult times. You can take solace that others are having a hard time meeting their budgets as well or you can change the way you deal with money in your congregation and actually wind up doing more for the Kingdom than ever before.

OTHER TOPICS

First Steps for the Newly Appointed Pastor

For many mainline clergy and churches, the early summer months are a time of transition. It is the time of year when new clergy, fresh from seminary, join the "real world" as pastors, and it is the month when seasoned clergy move to new churches. Most experienced pastors have a routine they like to follow when arriving at a new church, and a lot of churches have traditions they like to follow upon receiving a new pastor. I frequently see articles come out in May and June on best practices regarding assimilating. Seldom do I see anyone address financial stewardship and what one should do as soon as possible. It is a critical topic.

First, understand that financial stewardship does not need to be the absolute *first* thing you deal with. You need to focus on getting acquainted, learning where any urgent pastoral needs may be, and preparing for those first couple of Sundays when you need to be a combination of Billy Graham, Billy Sunday, and Pope Francis all at the same time. However, your to-do list needs to include learning all you can about the financial condition and practices of your church.

Occasionally a gifted clergyperson is awarded a fine new church to simply carry on the good work both have been doing. But oftentimes the clergyperson is told that the church is having serious problems (finances almost always mentioned) and told to go and fix the problem. In other words, "the bills aren't being paid, and we want

61

you to find a way to pay them." The message is clear: "Your ministry will be judged on whether you get the bills paid or not!" I will get several phone calls at the end of June or first of July with the question, "Hey, Clif, what do I do now?"

Here's what I would do if I were asked to do it over again: First, I would not ignore what I had been told about the church finances, but I would not make it my first priority, either. I would invest myself in learning about the ministry of this new church and exactly how they see themselves as the body of Christ:

- Do they understand the business they are in?

- Do they know that they are not the customer?

- Why do they have worship?

- How do they feel about their Sunday morning experience?

- What is their understanding of discipleship training?

- In what ways are they in mission outside their walls?

- What role does evangelism play in the life of this church?

- What shape are the youth and children's ministry areas in? Is there a sense of love and community here?

- How were key leaders put in place?

There is a real probability that in discovering the answer to these questions you will uncover the answer to why financial stewardship is as it is.

Second, I would find out where the greatest pastoral needs are for you to involve yourself in and begin immediately to be a pastor and a preacher. For the very large church this will mean discovering how your staff and key leaders need you to listen, love, and pray with them. For the smaller church this means discovering who is in the hospital, nursing home, or grieving over a loss. Persons need to know you want to love them as Christ loved us. Prepare those first three to four sermons with the realization that a large number of people will form lasting impressions of you and your leadership from what you say and how you say it.

Third, I would start doing my financial homework quietly and behind the scenes. Get lots of historical data on corporate and individual giving:

- Be sure and get data on annual, capital, and planned giving.

- See how things have evolved over the last several years. Do you see a trigger point when things radically changed for good or bad? Why?

- Talk with your financial leaders to get clarity (but avoid prescribing any solution), and also talk with those who have been your top donors to discover why they are supporting the church and what their expectations are.

- Talk to those who used to be key supporters and find out why they have chosen to move their support elsewhere.

- See if your elected leadership is also an invested leadership.

- See how your staff is exemplifying generosity.

Within the first couple of weeks I would schedule a visit with the church treasurer or business administrator and go over a series of questions:

- What is the current status of the church's finances?

- What are the trends that you have been seeing for the last couple of years?

- What has been customary here regarding the annual campaign, planned giving, and capital giving?

- What studies, if any, have been conducted regarding financial stewardship?

- What is shared with new members?

- Does the church have a unified budget or is there a capital budget as well?

- Exactly what happens after the offering is received with counting, recording, and reporting?

- When could I expect to get an updated report for the week?

- How often does the finance committee meet and what do they understand is their job and my job?

- Who has access to giving records?

How quickly can you get from the treasurer a list of last year's donors and a current list for this year that is in order of highest to lowest? You will want to spend time with this list on your own, deciphering what information you can. After looking it over you may want to go back to your finance person and get an understanding of exactly who some of those persons are and what their giving history has been like. Are your elected leaders also your best stewards? What can you discover about where their resources come from?

Then, I would schedule some informal visits with the top ten or so giving families. These are persons who have shown a willingness to make the church a high priority and they have been blessed with resources to make a real difference. You simply need to know them and know their hopes and dreams for the church. Are they tithers or just giving you a small portion of great wealth? Do they love Jesus or love control? Are they servants or do they want to be served? Can they be leaders or not? You need answers to all of these questions as you plan how best to accomplish your ministry strategy with your new church.

Six months into your tenure, call a retreat with no more than six to eight of your key leaders. Lay out what you have learned and lead a discussion on how you can better make disciples for Jesus Christ going forward. Make it a *ministry* discussion and not a *money* discussion. You aren't in the money business! Money will make its way into the discussion at the appropriate time, but ministry and changing lives needs to be the focus and intent. Very important—lead! Do not call this retreat and only listen. They have hired you to lead and God has called you to lead—do it!

Your goal is that at the end of your first year, you have a solid plan in place to go along with, hopefully, a high trust level from your people. Move forward with bold initiatives to make disciples. Then call your superior and tell him or her you have fixed the financial problem and the bills are paid.

What Pastors Learn from Members

Ministers often tell me they learn from their members. One of my favorite stories comes from the senior minister of an affluent suburban church with two thousand members. It happened during the church's lean start-up years, when they were meeting in a rented community facility. In the parking lot after the church service, the minister was approached as he was getting into his car by a church member in his early forties. The member pressed a check into his palm and explained that he recently sold the family business.

With tears in his eyes, this member shared that it meant a great deal to him to be able to make such a gift because the funds represented the fruits of his parents' hard work over several decades. He shared that he felt grateful to his parents for their strong faith and deep commitment to the community and the values they instilled in him, and he explained that he wanted to do the same for his children.

"I saw and felt the sincerity of his words at the moment and understood his deep need to make this gift," the minister said. "But it wasn't until I got into my car that I unfolded the check and saw that it was for $250,000. As a young pastor living on a modest salary, I could not even comprehend the numbers. I didn't trust my eyes."

Over the next few years, the minister witnessed how the power of making this gift transformed this member from a "dabbler" into a very committed Christian. This individual continued to start other companies that grew to be successful, and he continued to be very generous to the church. The minister concluded his story by telling me, "I learned from that experience that many members find great meaning in giving, and that my role as pastor is to graciously receive the gift and affirm the donor's generous spirit."

Some of my most memorable visits as a pastor were to my very generous members. I would find a convenient time, go sit in their den, and ask them to share with me why they gave as they did. I heard countless faith stories, fascinating journeys, and learned how they viewed money in their lives. I learned so much. During these visits I never asked for anything more than an explanation. Then I thanked them and almost always prayed with them prior to leaving.

What have you learned from your members? How do you graciously affirm the givers' generous spirits—or do you? Never underestimate your members' need to give as part of their journey of faith and the importance of your role in graciously affirming their generous spirits.

Best Practices for Money Handling in the Twenty-First Century

I have decided in my old age that playing a guitar and a banjo is exactly what I need to do to keep my brain sharp and to ease the stress that worrying about churches brings on. My guitar teacher told me the other day that he got his old turntable fixed so he could play his old 33 rpm records. He has a stack about six feet high. I am looking forward to hearing them. I have not heard music from a turntable in close to thirty years. I now get my music from the cloud and play it on my phone or iPod. I do have a few CDs left, but I have not bought one in quite some time.

The offering plate is going the way of the turntable. With each passing day and another funeral, in our churches we are seeing fewer and fewer persons who are comfortable putting cash in an envelope or writing a check for their weekly offering to the church. The baby boomers, Generation Xers, and millennials are far more comfortable giving with a credit card or debit card, using electronic transfer, or swiping at a kiosk than writing a check. However, the majority of our churches still put most of their emphasis, and in some instances their only emphasis, on putting a gift of cash or check in the plate. Where in the Bible does it say that is the only acceptable method? Then why do we not upgrade when it costs so little and can reap so much?

Every church with a website should have an easy and convenient way for persons to give online. Every church should share with their donors how they can easily set up an electronic transfer of funds on a regular schedule from their bank account to the church's account. Every church with a budget of $200,000 or more should have a readily accessible kiosk where donors can swipe a card just like at the gas station and give quickly and easily. Large churches should have a kiosk at every major entry point and multiple ones in the main narthex area. Most churches should now be using QR codes and credit card swipers.

I have nothing against checks or cash. I no longer carry a checkbook, and I carry very little cash, but I am fine with other people doing that. I have nothing against those who prefer to use those payment methods for their giving. I am also not opposed to people using turntables to listen to music. But if I really wanted to make money with music, I would not be producing it for turntables but utilizing every option available to me so that not just one segment of the population would buy my song, but everyone might buy my song.

Why are not more of our churches providing more means for people to give?

Bonds: The Basics and the Problems

Over the last couple of years a number of judicatories have asked if I could come in and work with a handful of their churches that they have identified as in trouble. It has been very gratifying but also very sad. The trouble they are in always relates to lack of money that frequently relates to one very bad decision. Sometimes we can fix the problem but often so many of the cows have left the barn that we have no hope of ever getting them back. Lately, many of these decisions seem to come from two sources: (1) selling bonds to finance an expansion and (2) starting a project prior to a campaign where persons would be asked to pay for it. Let me address bonds in this piece.

Bonds are quite simply just another way to borrow money. Instead of using a bank or other lending institution, the church uses a bond company to issue bonds that are usually then sold primarily to the church's members at an interest rate above what they can get in other fixed income assets. It is a good financial investment for the members, and so they buy the bonds and become the church's "bank." Several problems arise when this happens.

This year I have experienced a rash of calls regarding church bonds. It has been surprising because I have not had calls about selling bonds as a means of building in many years. For whatever reason, bonds have popped their head back up and pastors want information. Horizons does not sell bonds, and we do not have a relationship with anyone who does. In general, we do not feel that bonds are an effective or an appropriate method for churches to use for funds. In fact, we know many churches that are stuck with bonds and now wish they could rescind that decision.

Instead of getting a loan at a bank, the church makes a promissory note (bond) with all the persons who purchase the bonds. The promise to pay is still there. The church has just exchanged one lender for potentially hundreds. The selling of bonds is governed by individual states and sold through registered agents. This almost always means that a church will have to employ a commercial bonding company for a fee.

Bonds are either directed, sold to the members of the church generally by members of the church, or they are brokered and sold on the open market. Most church bonds are directed using the local church members as the purchasers (lenders).

The problems are numerous. First, church members can easily be lulled into believing they are practicing generosity, where in actuality they are not at all being generous. They are just moving investments to a guaranteed interest rate promised to them by their church. This rate is often higher than what persons can get on bonds in the marketplace, thus encouraging them to be bought. The selling of bonds can discourage members from giving and move them to lending. It changes the whole relationship of the church with its members. Encouraging your members to buy the church's bonds is not encouraging them to be generous donors or Kingdom builders. It is just offering them a good financial deal. It can even have a contrary effect on persons considering a sacrificial gift; they can come to feel that a loan and a gift really are the same thing. Your $100,000 gift can become a $50,000 gift and a $50,000 loan.

Second, bonds can make it very difficult to adjust payment schedules. Many churches have had to work with their bank to make adjustments from time to time. Others have had windfalls that enabled them to pay off a loan early. What happens if a person dies and leaves the church $1 million in their will? If you had a bank note you could quickly apply all of that to the principle and pay down your debt. But you have two hundred lenders and many of them do not want to receive a lump sum payoff ahead of schedule for tax or other reasons. They want to keep getting a high rate of return for the next decade. Do you try and force them to accept the payoff? Your church can easily become split as persons fight over what to do.

When you sell bonds you have a contract with often hundreds of lenders instead of one. Having many lenders makes adjustments very difficult. One church I know of has about forty members who are holding bonds that are paying 8 percent interest. The other members want to hold a campaign and pay these off, but the forty are standing firmly against it because they want a guaranteed return of 8 percent on their money. The conflict is tearing the church apart. In this economy, the church knows it could cut that interest rate in half with a bank loan, but the church leaders will not vote contrary to their best interests, and the church is paying out tens of thousands every year when it should not have to.

Another church we are working with wants to borrow more money, but they cannot because the bondholders are the primary mortgage holders. The banks will not lend their funds because they would be subordinate to the bondholders.

Bonds seem to only make sense when a solid lending institution (bank or denominational foundation) will not loan the funds. One church said the only way it could get money was to use a bonding company to sell bonds. First ask yourself, "Why will banks not loan the money?" They are in the lending business. However, they only want to make loans to those who will pay them back. What makes you a bad candidate? If banks do not feel you can repay a loan, have you bitten off more than you can chew? Will you be able to repay the bonds? Is it possible that you have no business borrowing that amount of money from anyone?

Do not overlook the up-front fees paid to the bonding company. They can be extremely high. A lending institution's closing costs are usually not even close to what is charged by bond firms.

Lastly, never sell bonds or borrow money from any source until you have run a campaign to see what your members might *give you.* A grant always beats a loan.

If you are thinking about bonds, think twice. It is an option, but generally, it is not a very good option.

Your Members and Their Taxes

Note: This essay was written at the end of 2010 and reflected on specific changes to tax law that would affect charitable donations. We are long past 2010/2011, but I included this essay to remind all church leaders that they are the recipients of charitable gifts from *donors*, not just members. Each year you should consult tax professionals about whether you need to communicate changes to your donors.

One survey I read found that more than 75 percent of financial advisors believed their clients would be subject to higher taxes in 2011. This is important for us in the church. Now, very few persons are motivated to give solely on the basis of a tax deduction, but with a great many affluent persons, it is certainly a consideration. These persons are continually looking ahead to the next year to try and position themselves in the best possible way for any increases that may come about. Well-run nonprofits are beginning to communicate with their donors early on about what may occur with taxes in the next year. The church needs to get in line by helping to educate our donors as well. October is a great month to do this. A number of things may occur with changes to the taxation structure:

Charitable Deduction Rates May Change

President Obama proposed in his 2011 budget that the maximum rate that could be used for a charitable deduction be 28 percent. Currently, the maximum rate that high-income persons can deduct is 33 or 35 percent, depending on their tax rate. A person who wanted to give away $100,000 would potentially save $7,000 by donating that money in 2010 rather than in 2011.

The Estate Tax Will Revert to 2001 Levels

There is no estate tax for anyone who dies in 2010, but in 2011 this all changed when Congress chose to reinstate the estate tax. This means that estates of $1 million or more could be taxed at a maximum rate of 55 percent. I am not advising you to encourage your members to die this year versus next year, but to remind them of the value of remembering the church in their will or creating a charitable trust arrangement that would remove assets from their estate and thus not burden loved ones with a potential tax bill that would only increase their grief.

Retirement Accounts

In 2010 people whose annual income exceeds $100,000 were allowed to convert some or all of their tax-deferred individual retirement accounts into a Roth IRA, which provides tax-free income in retirement. Because Roth IRAs are created with after-tax income, income taxes must be paid on the amount converted. Tax-smart donors could reduce the tax they owe on the conversion by making a charitable gift. A gift of assets not in one's regular cash flow, such as property or stock, may be a wise move for some.

It is important for all of our churches to share with their donors how gifts may help the church as well as benefit the donor throughout the year, but the last quarter of the year is the time when most persons are consulting advisors to ensure that they are tax prudent. I encourage all of you to consider getting a letter out this month advising your donors of these possible changes and encouraging a gift to the church. In your letter be very specific about how a gift could be used (i.e., strengthen the endowment fund, purchase playground equipment for children, fund a specific mission, buy a new church van, secure more nets for malaria, etc.). Help them see the *difference they can make*!

Before You "Fix," Examine Your Foundation

I must admit that at Horizons we get our fair share of callers who begin by telling us they are broke and need to be fixed. "We are 15 percent behind for the year and are about to lay off staff. Can you fix us?" "We have a big note payment due in a couple of months and no way to pay it. Can you fix us?" "Our building is falling down around us, and we can't afford to repair it. Can you fix us?"

The translation on this really should be, "Can you get us some *money?*" What I continue to discover is that the lack of money is what callers have most noticed, but it is not the cause of their problems nor will getting some more solve their problems. The biggest problem I see in these churches is that they have forgotten, if they ever knew, what a church was supposed to be doing in the first place. As they ceased to perform well as a church, their donors ceased to give well as participants. Too many churches today are operating on shaky ground, forgetting to examine their own foundation.

I read an article the other day about a speech Dr. Steve Perry gave. Dr. Perry is a very innovative educator from Hartford, Connecticut. His schools have Saturday classes, a longer school year, and no summer break, and every student is expected to go to college. The population the school serves is poor urban students. And for the last three years every single one of his graduates has indeed gone on to college. Here is some of what he said:

"There's no point in trying to 'reform' schools that can't be reformed. It's better to shut 'em down, let 'em go, cut 'em loose—and start a good school. One that's serious about educating kids."

"I have seen, for far too long, teachers keeping their jobs without putting out educated children," and "If a school does not educate, it's not a school."[1]

Now just substitute the word *church* for *school*. What expectations are made perfectly clear to persons who come into your church about how they are to contribute to being the body of Christ? Is there any accountability?

What happens to a church that has not had a profession of faith (new convert) in years? Is it still allowed to absorb resources and call itself a church? How does it contribute to bringing in the kingdom of God? What is the reason to keep a place as a church if persons are not discovering Christ in that place? Would it be better to shut it down?

What about a pastor who has not led anyone to Christ in years? The pastor preaches without passion or conviction. The church being saved is not producing any noticeable fruit. There are fewer and fewer seats being occupied for worship. He or she occupies a spot and takes up time and resources and produces what? Should we be replacing him or her as soon as possible?

An overwhelming number of our churches are indeed broke, but the problem is not money. The problem is that they have forgotten what it is to be a church. Alternative schools are springing up all over because so many of our public institutions are not educating. People are leaving the church and ceasing to give money because lives are not being changed or transformed.

As you begin the new year many persons may be encouraging you to change what you do with money because the church is broke. To fix money problems, you may need to change how you do church. Do something truly radical next year. Be the body of Christ to the world around you.

The Power of Saying Thanks

One of the great shortcomings of church leadership is that we do not come close to expressing thanks to our donors in comparison to other nonprofits. For instance, I just finished a year in which my family gave more money to the church than in any previous year. We were one of the top contributors to our church, yet I did not get a thank-you note. About two weeks ago I sent a small check to my alma mater. Within five days I got a handwritten thank-you. Now I still love my church, and I will still give generously to the church, but what about someone who is not quite as connected as I am? Will they compare the difference in response of one nonprofit to another? Many certainly will.

Before the end of the year start doing two things:

First, have your board call every family that made a contribution in the last year and thank them. To do this divide the families up among the board members and ask them to make their calls within a one-week period. They should do this before the end of the year.

Second, pastors should start writing ten to fifteen thank-you notes a week to donors and others who have made a considerable difference in the church. This will take only twenty to thirty minutes, but the response will be overwhelming. One pastor who has already started this practice told me the other day, "I wrote ten the first week. On Sunday one of the older men of the church to whom I had written stopped me in the hall and said that in all his years in the church he had never gotten a handwritten note from his pastor. Then he thanked me!" If church leadership would thank the members two times more than it does and beg from them only half as much, I am convinced that contributions of money and time would go up markedly.

I got a call near the end of the year from one of my client pastors wanting to know if he should make a solicitation call to a new family that had given $30,000 at the end of the previous year. I told him no, but my advice was for him to stop by their home, thank them profusely for the gift last year, and then specifically invite them to be a part of something upcoming at the church. I also encouraged him to talk with them about how the church can better serve them. He was not to mention one thing about an end-of-the-year gift. He decided to go with my approach, and he called me the week before Christmas to report that the wife of the family came in with a check for $85,000 and asked him to come back out and talk some more about how they could be more involved. I told him to go after he sat down and wrote a long thank-you note.

When Members Threaten to Withhold

One financial question I am often asked is, "How do you handle persons who say that unless certain changes are made, they will not give to the church?" This occurs in most churches in America on an all-too-frequent basis, and it certainly occurred to me in every church that I served.

First, make sure you have a clear understanding of what the person or persons are saying. It is important to get your facts right. Sometimes there is simply a misunderstanding about what is factual, and correcting a false interpretation can resolve the matter.

Second, look at yourself and see if you have made a mistake. I do not condone the "withholding tactic" or threats, but it is possible you need to apologize. Now understand, the person withholding money for his or her demands should apologize for his or her behavior as well, but what that person chooses to do does not determine the course of action you should take. If you messed up, own it and say, "I am sorry."

Third, assuming that the facts are right and what you, or the church, did was very intentional and you feel the correct action was taken, then the issue is simply control—and they want it! Most of the time these types of threats are issued by persons who merely want to get their way. Their attitude is that the church is there to serve them and they do not feel properly served by the actions taken, so they will not pay. This is much like customers not paying when they do not get what they ordered from a restaurant. You cannot mold the church, the body of Christ, around the whims of single individuals. We are in the disciple-making business, not the appeasement-making business. You must attempt to get the debate to shift to *mission*. Was the action taken on behalf of the mission? Could the action others preferred have accomplished the same thing for the mission? Which course is best for making disciples for Jesus Christ? This must become the debate. If others do not want to engage in that discussion, then you just do not engage. *They* are not your *mission*. They did not die on the cross for our salvation. They are not the Messiah. They are not the ones we call Lord. It is about Jesus!

We all need to understand that anyone can choose at any time to give or not to give to anything he or she wishes. In the church, we do not want people to give because they have an obligation but because they are so grateful for what God has given them. If they do not want to do that, then that is their choice. You are not responsible for their choices. You, as a church leader, are responsible for your job of making disciples of Jesus Christ for the transformation of the world. Never forsake the mission! Do not do it for $10 or $10,000 or $10 million. The mission is first. Not you, not them, not anybody—the mission!

A last note: While you are losing sleep over this threat, go look at what these persons are actually giving. Usually, you sleep better after that.

Two Things I See in Churches with Great Giving

I have gotten many positive responses to my book *Rich Church, Poor Church* and I am appreciative. The book covers much of what I have seen in churches that have excellent records in financial stewardship. The book covers almost exclusively issues around the policies and practices regarding money. Not every church I lifted up does everything that I highlighted, but they do most things. I think it is also helpful and important to consider what I have consistently seen in a church with outstanding financial stewardship. These are two things I see in churches with great givers (and great records of giving):

High-Quality Sunday Morning Worship

Persons come to church to be lifted up from ordinary life. They come to feel a connection with the one who is above and beyond all. They come seeking hope and renewal. They come wanting to know they are not alone. Worship in churches with great stewardship sends persons home with more than they came in with. These worship services do not leave one stone unturned in achieving excellence. The music is outstanding. The sermon is motivating and stimulating. There is no dead space where people wait while others move into position. The videos and sound are top notch. Every single minute of this experience is given the due it deserves to ensure that persons who enter leave feeling like they have touched the face of God. You just cannot have excellent financial stewardship and poor worship at the same time.

A Connected Staff

If the staff of the church is not 100 percent behind the senior pastor, where all are on the same page seeking to lead the church in a common direction, there will be turmoil if not chaos. This will then be reflected in poor financial stewardship results. Way too often the attention goes to money when the problem is in the staff. Very few churches will have all their laity on the same page, but you can have laity discord and still have a very healthy church with excellent stewardship. If and when you have disconnect within the professional staff, however, you will in very short order have an atmosphere where people do not want to invest. All staff persons must give total loyalty to the leader as long as that leader is moral and ethical. Disagreements and discussions can and should be held between staff and leader, but when the day is done, staff is either loyal or they may choose to no longer be staff. You will never achieve financial stewardship success if you cannot get the staff and pastor on the same page.

I work with hundreds of churches every year and most call, e-mail, or ask me to come because they do not have enough money at the end of the day and the bill collectors are at their door. They say things like, "You need to help us get persons who do not give to give"; or "We would be fine if we could just get this mortgage off our books"; or "Too many of our families are just over committed to a new house and other stuff. How do we get them to give us more money?"

Are you sure your problem is money? How good is your worship? How united is your staff?

Selecting Members and Leaders for Your Finance Team

The vast majority of all churches have persons who serve on the finance committee or finance team or some other committee that deals with the budget, revenue, and often pledges. These groups are constructed differently, varying from a leadership team (deacons or elders in some churches) to a separately elected group that frequently has a three-year rotation system. Regardless, no one is born into this position. They are asked to serve by someone for some reason. In too many of these churches, it is for the wrong reason.

Most of the time when I inquire as to why some people were chosen to serve on the finance team, the answer is that they know a lot about money. They are bankers or stockbrokers or CPAs or insurance agents and deal intimately with money matters every day. Thus, they are the best qualified to serve in this way in the church. Bad answer!

Now I have nothing against bankers or CPAs. I have a son who is a CPA and a son-in-law who is a banker. Both are fine men and both are active churchmen. However, it is not their professional skills that would most qualify them to serve their churches. It is their spiritual maturity that should first be determined. The church is *not* in the money business. We are in the *Jesus* business. Our profit is measured not so much in a balanced budget but in disciples made for Jesus. Our bottom line is different than a corporation or a bank. Anyone who advises on expenditures needs to first and foremost understand and totally buy in to our mission. What you need to ascertain prior to asking people to serve in such a powerful place is the answer to the following question: Do they know the mission and will they use their skills to help make disciples as their first priority? If all they know is money, then you do not want or need them in this position.

No one should serve in the financial capacity of a church who does not show strong evidence of being a steward in his or her use of personal resources. That person is, after all, being asked to lead others in this experience of the Christian faith. What sort of example does he or she set? What sort of integrity will he or she bring from the recommendations of others? Is Jesus or money the real lord?

The tithe was my standard for anyone who served on the finance team in my churches. I had a covenant that each was asked to review prior to accepting a position. The covenant stated that he or she would pray on a regular basis for the church, attend every Sunday they were healthy and able, be a part of one service group working outside the walls of the church, and tithe. Some would look at the covenant and politely decide that this team was not for them, but most would sign and fulfill it to the letter. It gave us a team with great integrity with everyone on the same page as decisions were made. At least I could feel that the team members understood the mission and were committed to it. Money never took precedence over mission.

How do you assemble leaders for this team? Are you certain in their commitment to Christ by the evidence you can see? Will they be working to move the church closer to the cross or just a balanced budget?

How to Begin Your Yearly Budget

Every church I know of has a budget. It may be a half page in a small church or multiple pages in a large one, but everyone has a budget. It has always struck me that though all churches have one and every pastor is often tasked with preparing one, no class was ever held in "pastor training school" on how to do it.

One of the best books for any pastor to help in this arena is *Ministry and Money* by Janet T. and Philip D. Jamieson. In doing finances in the church, this book should be viewed as a primer by every pastor and sit on every desk. But apart from so many helpful chapters in this book, I want to offer you the place where you should always start in preparing the budget: your church's mission. What is it that the funds flowing into your church should do?

As you look over the previous year's budget, look at each and every line and ask these questions:

- How does this enable us to fulfill our mission?

- Will putting money in this category bring a return on the investment in accomplishing what we are in business to do?

- Is it possible to get the same return by spending less money?

- Will we get a greater return toward our mission if we spend more?

- If this position was not in our budget, exactly how would it measurably affect our mission?

- If this position had a higher or lower salary, how would it measurably affect our mission?

- How would our members respond if this item was not in the budget but presented as a designated giving opportunity? Do they see the value in what is being done? Why or why not?

- How would we feel if we took the items in our budget and presented them to the Lord as evidence of what we have chosen to do with the talents he gave us?

- What is not in the budget that is crying out to be added as an expenditure that would significantly affect our mission performance?

Far too often we look at the church budget as a financial document. It is a spiritual evidence sheet! On those pages people should be able to determine why you are in business and how spiritually in tune you are with God's call in your life. The worst thing you can do is just say that the budget should go up or down by a certain percent. From the electric bill to the janitor's salary—all get judged on the mission!

Special Offerings on Christmas Eve

Christmas and Easter are opportunities to maximize the increase in your church's attendance, to make a real difference in the lives of those who attend—and in the lives of many other people. As a case study (and inspiration), I want to share what I witnessed at one very smart church's Christmas Eve service. They did everything right when it came to stewardship. It is worth saying that the entire service was extremely well done with the music and message, but my job is stewardship so I will report to you on that. Here are the four things they did well:

The offering was totally dedicated to those outside the church walls. Upon entering, I received a bulletin and in it was an insert with an explanation of the ministry that was going to receive 100 percent of the offering. The church was aware that it would have a number of visitors who would not necessarily feel comfortable giving to a local church, especially if they already belonged to one as is frequently the case on Christmas Eve with out-of-town visitors. Those same persons, however, may want to make an expression of gratitude on Christmas.

A video was produced to explain how lives are being changed through this outside ministry and shown right before the offering. God sent God's only Son into the world that lives might be changed through him. This video helped me and others to see exactly how lives were being changed through this wonderful ministry that would be supported by our offering. In fact, it was so good I doubled my intended offering as a way of saying thanks to this God of love. I could really see in the video how I could partner with God to change even more lives, and I was excited to do it.

A QR code was printed in the bulletin for anyone to use with their smart phone to make a gift. I watched as the person next to me took out his smartphone, used his code reader, and scanned the code in the bulletin. It took him to the church website that had a large lead-in to the Christmas Eve offering. The gentleman put in his credit card number, hit send, and made a contribution in less than one minute. I looked around the sanctuary and saw several others doing the same thing. How ingenious this was. I had not thought of using QR codes in this way, but it was so easy. It was also right inside the wheelhouse of many in that congregation. The man next to me looked to be in his early thirties and using his smart phone to make a contribution was a common occurrence for him.

People were told how to make a contribution to the local church if they so desired. The attenders were told that envelopes were in the pew backs if they wished to make a contribution to this church. The leaders knew that some members would be present who wanted to make an end-of-the-year gift, and a method was provided for them to do just that, however, any funds placed in the plate and not in the envelope would go to the specified mission outside of the church.

This church was smart because they gave *everyone the best chance to give.* Most churches give appeals that only members will respond to or only those with cash in their wallet or only those who are over sixty. This church was smart, and you, too, can be this church.

Postscript on a
New Perspective

Hello, God, it's Clif. We need to talk. Things are really bad, and I am just a little bit afraid. The world around me just seems to be a real mess, and I don't know where to turn but to you. I hope you have time to listen.

For the third day in a row I have lost a lot of money in the stock market. I am down nearly 15 percent from where I was just a week ago, and if you want to throw in the week prior to that it is even worse. Lord, I don't want to work forever. I would like to retire. I have this plan, and it is all messed up today. I don't know if I ought to buy, sell, or stay put. Please, Lord, what can I say?

My air conditioner quit working last Sunday afternoon, and it was 104 degrees outside. Now, Lord, that is hot. When the house gets hot, it makes it hard to sleep or study or think. This wasn't a bill I had counted on having to pay either. Have you had to get an air conditioner repairperson lately on a Sunday? Please, Lord, what can I say?

I was on my way to the office when one of those little dashboard lights came on that said I have a problem. Oh, no! With the market down and the air conditioner broken, now my truck is in need of some work. When I got it to the repair shop they told me it would be $750. Where does that come from? I thought this truck was warranted for 100,000 miles but apparently not for this repair. Please, Lord, what can I say?

I got out of bed last week and felt a sharp pain up my leg. It came from my heel. Man, it really hurt. Do you know what it is like to have a nail in your foot? Yeah, I forgot; I guess you do. Anyway, I went to the foot specialist and got a special orthotic for "only" $500. My foot is feeling better, but gosh I don't like feeling like stuff is breaking all the time. Please, Lord, what can I say?

That foot stuff was not nearly as bad as waking up and having half my tooth break off while eating cereal. Right... cereal. Not exactly crunching ice. It was just Cheerios, and now I have this big hole in my mouth where a tooth used to be. I don't even want to tell you what a crown costs, but let's just say it was worse than the foot. Please, Lord, what can I say?

I guess I am done, though I have a lot more I could tack on. Any word on this?

THE LORD: Nice to hear from you, Clif.

You might start with "thank you, Lord, that I have any money to lose and that I can even ask such ridiculous questions like buy, sell, or stay put." Then you could move on to "thank you, Lord, that I have a house. Air conditioning is a nice thing, I am sure, but do you know how many persons in the world don't even have a house?"

I am sorry your truck had a part that broke, but after 80,000 miles some human-made parts do break. How many vehicles do you own now? Is it two or three? How about a "thank you, Lord, that I don't have to walk everywhere"?

Your feet hurt, too. It is amazing how you humans have trouble with stuff that my chimps and gorillas never seem to struggle with. My fault or yours? Anyway, it might make you feel better if you went over to the VA and visited some of my children who are fighting for your freedom in Afghanistan. They don't have any feet left to hurt.

I am sure that having a tooth break off was traumatic for you. How many different dentists did you find available to you in the Yellow Pages? What a blessing that such persons exist for you. Do you know that there are a lot of countries that don't have as many in the entire nation as you have in your little town?

Why don't you just start your next conversation with "thank you, Lord" and then go from there. This new perspective might help you out a bit.

This has been a wonderful conversation, Clif. It just reminded me of how blessed you really are. Now what else do you want to say?

RECOMMENDED READING

I am constantly being asked to recommend books on finance and stewardship to pastors and persons in the church. Generally my first response is to ask people what topics they are looking for. Below is a list of books I have read and the categories I would place them under. I hope that helps you find texts that will assist you in growing into a stewardship leader in your church. Most, if not all, are available on the major online book outlets. These are also the books that are recommended by the Horizons Stewardship Academy of Faith and Money.

Today's Stewardship Realities

Christopher, J. Clif. *Not Your Parents' Offering Plate: A New Vision for Financial Stewardship*. Nashville: Abingdon Press, 2008.
———. *Whose Offering Plate Is It?* Nashville: Abingdon Press, 2010.
These companion texts lay out an argument on why the church can no longer do stewardship as it has been doing it for half a century. The need to compete around why people give is thoroughly emphasized. *Whose Offering Plate Is It?* offers a list of practical ways to implement the strategies outlined in the initial best-selling volume.

———. *Rich Church, Poor Church: Keys to Effective Financial Ministry*. Nashville: Abingdon Press, 2012.
The book is designed to get groups of church leaders to examine their congregation to see if their practices are similar to the Rich Church (one that has all the money necessary to focus on mission and ministry) or the Poor Church (one that must concentrate on

money each day so as to pay its bills). It will promote excellent group discussion and can be a catalyst for healthy change to get a Poor Church to become a Rich Church.

Miller, Kristine, and Scott McKenzie. *Bounty: Ten Things You Can Do Now to Increase Giving at Your Church*. Nashville: Abingdon Press, 2013.

This is an excellent book for a church finance committee to study. It lays out how giving to the church has changed dramatically and how donors think differently today than yesterday. Some good practical strategies are also included. Good group study guide.

Theology of Stewardship

Nouwen, Henri. *A Spirituality of Fundraising*. Nashville: Upper Room Books, 2010.

If I could have every pastor only read one book on the theology of stewardship, this is it. For those who somehow think that money should not be a part of their ministry or spiritual life, this is a must-read. It is also extremely short. You can read and digest this book in one hour!

Finances and Running the Church

Searcy, Nelson. *Maximize: How to Develop Extravagant Givers in Your Church*. With Jennifer Dykes Henson. Grand Rapids: Baker Books, 2010.

Searcy is the lead pastor of The Journey Church of the City. This book is absolutely chock-full of useful ideas that have proven successful for Searcy and his churches. It is easy to read and lays out a framework for growing persons in generosity. I loved this book.

Jamieson, Janet T., and Philip D. Jamieson. *Ministry and Money: A Practical Guide for Pastors*. Lexington: Westminster John Knox Press, 2009.

Malphurs, Aubrey, and Steve Stroope. *Money Matters in Church: A Practical Guide for Leaders.* Grand Rapids: Baker Books, 2007.

Both of these books should be required reading in every seminary. They are extremely practical with strong legal and theological premises for why and how we do financial stewardship in the church. If I had read these books forty years ago, I would have been a much better pastor. If you read them now, you will be far more prepared going forward.

Fund-Raising Principles

Panas, Jerold. *Born to Raise.* Chicago: Pluribus Press, 1988.
———. *Mega Gifts: Who Gives Them, Who Gets Them?* 2nd ed. Medfield, MA: Emerson & Church, 2005.

Panas is a giant in the fund-raising profession and many a great fund-raiser grew up on his writings and teachings. Both of these books are fundamental and groundbreaking. They are not written for the church, but any good church leader can translate the nonprofit language to church language and see how to apply the advice.

Rosso, Henry A. *Rosso on Fund Raising: Lessons from a Master's Lifetime Experience.* San Francisco: Jossey-Bass Publishers, 1996.

This is another foundational book written for fund-raisers by one of the greatest fund-raisers of the last century. It is easy to read and covers the topic very well.

Preaching and Stewardship

Satterlee, Craig A. *Preaching and Stewardship: Proclaiming God's Invitation to Grow.* Herndon, VA: Alban Institute, 2011.

For those who struggle to preach on money with power and to get a congregation to listen with earnestness, this is the book.

Tennant, Matthew. *Preaching in Plenty and in Want.* Valley Forge, PA: Judson Press, 2011.

So many of our pastors find themselves surrounded not by the poor but by those who represent the top 1 to 2 percent of wealth in the world. Our churches are full of persons with plenty who want more. Preach to them, brothers and sisters.

Major Gifts and Asking

Panas, Jerold. *Asking: A 59-Minute Guide to Everything Board Members, Volunteers, and Staff Must Know to Secure the Gift.* Medfield, MA: Emerson & Church, 2013.

This book will take you about one hour to read, and when you are done you will know exactly how one of the world's great fundraisers does an *ask.* It directly applies to the church and nonprofits alike.

Collier, Charles W. *Wealth in Families.* 3rd ed. Boston: President and Fellows of Harvard College, 2012.

To help persons use their wealth as stewards, we have to understand how this wealth came to be, how the possessors feel about it, and how they feel about giving it away.

Planned Giving

Reeves, Michael, Rob Fairly, and Sanford Coon. *Creative Giving: Understanding Planned Giving and Endowments in Church.* Nashville: Discipleship Resources, 2005.

If a church leader will read this excellent book that is written just for them, they will know all they need to know about planned gifts.

Authors I Always Want to Read

Bill Easum
Adam Hamilton
Mike Slaughter
Andy Stanley

I have been reading books these faith giants have written for over a decade, and I have not regretted a single one of them. Some are directly about money and many are not, but every one of them has made me a better pastor and steward. If you see their names on a book and you have not read it, buy the book!

Visit http://www.cokesbury.com/forms/digitalstore. aspx?lvl=free+downloads to download a free PDF of sample resources for your church. Password: So2u686s0Y

NOTES

The State of the Church and Finance

1. Holly Hall, "Fiscal Crisis Reshaped How Donors Give," *The Chronicle of Philanthropy* 25, no. 19 (September 26, 2013).

2. *Giving USA: The Annual Report on Philanthropy for the year 2011* (2012). Chicago: Giving USA Foundation, www.givingUSAreports.org.

3. Ibid.

Large Gifts, Endowments, and Planned Giving

1. *Planned Giving in the United States 2000: A Survey of Donors* (Partnership for Philanthropic Planning, 2000).

The Church's Expectations of Its Members

1. Tom Bandy, forward to *Beyond the Collection Plate*, by Michael Durall (Nashville: Abingdon Press, 2003).

2. Christie Storm, "More Mormons," *Little Rock, Arkansas Democrat-Gazette*, December 12, 2009.

Doom-Saying

1. Penelope Burk, *The Cygnus Donor Survey... Where Philanthropy Is Headed in 2010* (Chicago: Cygnus Applied Research, 2010).

The Power of Purpose

1. Cathleen Falsani, "A Shopping Spree to Save Earth," *Orange County Register* (Santa Ana, CA), April 23, 2013.

Tithing and How to Lead It

1. Nelson Searcy, *Maximize: How to Develop Extravagant Givers in Your Church*, with Jennifer Dykes Henson (Grand Rapids: Baker Books, 2010).

Help for the Hard Times

1. The Barna Group, "The Economy's Impact (Part 3 of 3): Donors Reduce Giving, Brace for the Long Haul," *Barna Update*, February 8, 2010.

Other Topics

1. "A Reformer Speaks; But Who's Listening to Him?," *Little Rock, Arkansas Democrat-Gazette,* January 21, 2011, http://www.kipp.org/index.cfm?objectid=28AC2A30-2583-11E0-8355005056883C4D.